The Charm Syndrome

Sandra Horley grew up in Sarnia, Ontario, in Canada. She worked as a secretary in Montreal and then received a scholarship to study sociology at McGill University. She has also studied at the universities of Oxford and Birmingham.

In 1979 she took up her first job in the field of woman abuse as organiser of the Haven project in Wolverhampton. Since 1983 she has been director of Chiswick Family Rescue. She has also worked as a counsellor for abused women, as a homelessness officer in Shrewsbury, and as a housing advice worker in Brixton.

A committed campaigner on behalf of battered women, she gave evidence to the Metropolitan Police Working Party on Domestic Violence in 1985. She currently trains police, health, housing and social workers, and gives frequent talks and broadcasts.

Sandra Horley's first book, *Love and Pain: A Survival Handbook for Women*, was published in 1988 by Bedford Square Press. She lives in north London with her photographer husband, Julian, and their daughter Samantha.

The Charm Syndrome

Why Charming Men Can
Make Dangerous Lovers

Sandra Horley

Director, Chiswick Family Rescue

PAPERMAC

First published in 1991 by
PAPERMAC
a division of Macmillan Publishers Limited
4 Little Essex Street London WC2R 3LF
and Basingstoke

Associated companies in Auckland, Delhi, Dublin, Gaborone,
Hamburg, Harare, Hong Kong, Johannesburg, Kuala Lumpur,
Lagos, Manzini, Melbourne, Mexico City, Nairobi, New York,
Singapore and Tokyo

ISBN 0-333-45669-6

A CIP catalogue record for this book is available from the British Library

Typeset by Macmillan Production Limited

Printed in Hong Kong

Note: While the examples in this book are based on real
cases, individuals' details, including names, events, injuries,
occupations, etc., have been changed to conceal their
identities and to protect their families. Any resemblance
to other people is purely coincidental.

Every effort has been made to trace all copyright holders
but if any has been inadvertently overlooked the authors and
publishers will be pleased to make the necessary arrangement
at the first opportunity.

He is
   charming,
      so,
         be sure
            that you
            keep him like fire
            beyond the tips of your fingers.
                  (Diane Wakoski, 'The Catalogue of Charms')

This book is for my family:

for my husband, Julian, who taught me that men can be loving, caring and non-sexist; for my daughter, Samantha, and her contemporaries, in the hope that they will live in a better world; for my mother, whose encouragement made me want to fight injustice.

Contents

Acknowledgements

This book could not have been written without the contributions of many abused women who bravely shared their stories with me. To them my deepest gratitude.

A very special thanks to Sheila Keating for working so hard to help me get my ideas on paper. Her quick grasp of the material, organisational ability and writing talent helped make this book a reality.

A big thank-you to Jess Curtis, who assisted in the initial stages of this book and who has been a silent supporter over the years.

Various friends and colleagues have helped me by providing support, ideas and inspiration: Colin Brown; Dr Susan Edwards; Al Cove; Jackie Sallon (Bedford Square Press); Annie Ware; Jurgen Dankwort; Harold and Nancy Ship; Alison Strode; Paul Nieman; Rose Howard; Walter Easey; Bev Lever; Libba Davies; David and Deborah Sinclair; Sue Coleman (organiser, The Haven Project); Superintendent Paul Green, Inspector J. Duncan Wilson, Inspector Jane Stitchbury, Sergeant Colette Paul, and WPC Jayne Vickers of the Metropolitan Police.

I am very grateful to Walter Bealby, barrister (and friend), for his generous help and advice (and for his jokes).

My special gratitude to Fred Mashaal for twenty years of friendship and encouragement. Also to Evelyn Kolish and Cynthia Taylor for their sensitive support and long-distance reassurance; to Ruby Brooke for her words of wisdom and support whilst this book was being written; and to Mary Russell for her very sound advice and friendship.

I would like to express my appreciation to all at Chiswick Family Rescue. In particular, I would like to thank Mary Finn for acting as a sounding-board for ideas and sharing the work at Chiswick Family Rescue during the past five years; Philomena Gallear, whose commitment and care for abused women has taught me so much; Peter Wallach, who is an active ally in the struggle against woman abuse; Karen and Pete Townshend for their continued support; and Neville Vincent, who taught me about people and contributed more to the women's movement than can ever be acknowledged.

My appreciation goes to Carol Smith, my literary agent. Also to Katrina Whone, my editor, whose comments and support proved invaluable in the latter stages of this book. Peter James did an excellent job copy-editing the final manuscript.

I thank Shirley Jane Horley, my mother, for her warmth, her courage and her remarkable spirit of survival. She taught me to believe in myself and to persevere against all odds.

There is no way I can adequately thank Aileen, my mother-in-law, for her tireless loyalty and support. Her assistance was so often asked for and so freely given.

Thank you to Nesia Tapit, who cheerfully kept our household going and helped look after our daughter, Samantha, while this book was being written.

I am especially grateful to my husband, Julian, who was consistently supportive, loving and encouraging during the difficult years while this book was in progress. Finally, to 'Sam', our daughter, who tolerated the closed door of my study and yet remains a joy.

A Personal Introduction

I was prompted to write this book by one woman in particular, a woman whose husband never hit her or even threatened to hit her, but who made her life a living hell for twenty-five years. When they first met, he was the perfect gentleman, a complete charmer. At dinner parties he was the life and soul of the group. Her best friend thought he was terrific. Her mother thought he was the great provider. Everyone thought she was so lucky.

But after they were married, she began to see a different side of him. Gradually he managed to cut her off from her friends – though at the time she hardly noticed what was happening. He began to turn down invitations to dinner parties they had once enjoyed. Sometimes, if they did see other people, he would very subtly put her down, laugh at her opinions or make her feel like a fool in front of them, often in ways only she understood, leaving her feeling uncomfortable.

Afterwards, if she was upset, he would put his arm around her and say things like: 'You know I was only teasing, darling. Don't take it so personally.' Then he would be attentive and considerate again, and enthusiastic about their life together. He would tell her that they could not live without each other, that he needed her, that nobody else had what they had. If she talked to friends about her niggles over his behaviour, they could not understand what was worrying her. As far as they could see he was a kind, caring man. Everyone has their problems, they agreed, but that was all there was to it.

For long periods everything would be 'normal' and peaceful but then he would do or say something which would completely throw her. When she decided to do something for herself, to take up some part-time studying at home, he was so outraged that he burnt her lifetime's collection of diaries, drawings and books in the fire.

When she was in hospital having their first child, she waited every day for him to visit, but he never came. Then, when she brought the baby home, she opened the living-room door to find the word 'slut' traced in the thin layer of dust on the coffee table which had accumulated while she was away.

Mortified as she was, she bit her tongue, because she wanted them to be happy with the new baby.

But his moods became more unpredictable. If his dinner was not on the table when he came home, or she was talking to a friend on the telephone, he could be angry and abusive, or cold and distant. He made all the decisions, and expected her to accept them without question. When she stood up for herself, and tried to develop outside interests, he even threatened to have her committed to a mental home. There must be something wrong with her, he argued, if she was not happy looking after him and her children. Why did she need anything else?

Their friends were like his echoes. They could not see why she seemed discontented. Unwittingly they made her feel that it must be her fault if she was not happy. She got tired of people starting sentences with 'But he's so nice . . . ', implying that she was some sort of dragon, that she was on edge, snappy and irritable.

This woman is not alone. In my twelve years as a counsellor, I have realised that her misery is shared by many, many women, who may have no cuts, bruises or scars, but who only know that they are miserable in their relationships. Many women are immobilised by the effects of years and years of subtle, all-pervading emotional and verbal abuse, without ever thinking of themselves as abused at all. Surely that is something which happens to other people?

Many of these women seem to be strong, confident, capable people. Some are qualified professional women, who appear to have perfect marriages and relationships. No one knows that deep down they feel unfulfilled and dissatisfied, not knowing why the control they exercise over their job is lacking in their relationship with their partner. With him they continually mind their ps and qs and alter their behaviour to make life more tolerable. They are unable to be themselves.

Yet should anyone suggest that they are abused, they would say, 'Don't be silly.' Even if there are things that disturb them, they frequently gloss over them, make excuses for their partner's behaviour, or convince themselves that they are imagining things, often because they cannot bear to admit either to themselves or to colleagues and friends that their relationship is less than wonderful. After all, they are married to the most charming man in the world. If they complain to friends who see their partner only as a nice friendly guy, they run the risk of appearing to do nothing but put their husband or boyfriend down. Often the result is that the man ends up with all the sympathy.

Often, too, the incidents which worry them seem so trivial when taken on their own. Many women who ring the Refuge begin by apologising for asking for help over something which they think sounds silly. They do not believe they have the right to ask for assistance when they have no physical wounds to show for their distress. One women rang me, saying, 'I shouldn't really be calling you. I'm probably wasting your time. I'm not really one of your women. He doesn't hit me, but I know there's something wrong with our relationship . . .'

What such women are unaware of, since they do not even realise that they are being abused, is that their desperation and confusion, their low self-esteem, is a direct result of their partner's abusive behaviour.

Do not think for a moment that I am dismissing the hundreds of women who come to see me with hideous wounds, women who are literally scared for their lives. A recent London survey showed that the problem of woman abuse is horrifyingly high (I prefer to talk about 'woman abuse', rather than 'wife abuse', as women who live with their partners but do not marry them are as much at risk as wives).

One in four women has been hit by her partner, and Canadian research shows that women are beaten thirty-five times before they contact the police for help.

One of the few men who has actually come forward and admitted his violence (in a television programme on woman abuse) revealed that, out of eleven of his friends, every one had hit a woman at some time. This guy was everybody's idea of the boy next door – to him such behaviour was the norm. Eighteen per cent of all murders are committed by men on their female partners, and over 1000 women contact the Metropolitan Police for help every week.

Headline news and figures such as these only highlight the more sensational stories – but scalded limbs, broken bones, wounds from knives and hatchets and murder threats are not the only legacies of the abuser. Emotional and mental abuse leaves scars as deep as physical wounds. And many women live with such abuse *as well* as physical batterings.

Many of the women I talk to in my work are so continually degraded, demoralised and humiliated by their partners that they have lost all confidence in themselves. They feel constantly undermined by their partners. They are depressed and confused. What is more they feel terribly alone. Because they have no bruises to show, they think no one will understand.

I wanted to know why so many women are abused – both physically and emotionally. I wanted to know why men think they have the right to behave in such a controlling, domineering way towards their partners. I talked to hundreds of women, and delved into reams of research on abused women and the men who abuse them. The result is this book – my attempt to explain why men abuse women. I hope to show that the predominant reason why men behave in this way is because we live in a society which, frankly, allows – indeed encourages – them to do so. A society which bombards us with messages that men are dominant and powerful, and that women are nothing without them, that they are dependent on them for their sense of self-worth and security. A society which makes it hard for women who want to leave their abusers to find houses, jobs, childcare and so on. A society which implies that they bring it on themselves. 'She must have provoked it,' people say.

I should add that in stressing the role of society, I am not dismissing individual psychological factors in woman abuse, but they are factors, not causes. My concern is to show that woman abuse is a *pattern* of behaviour – men who abuse behave in remarkably similar ways – as indeed do women who receive abuse. We can learn to recognise this pattern, and in doing so we will see how it is the product of social conditioning.

As Emmeline Pankhurst observed, 'As a river cannot flow higher than its source, so a society cannot be judged higher than the way it treats its women.' Well, despite the great strides that women have made since Emmeline Pankhurst made her stand, women are still devalued and discriminated against. And if we go on implying that women are not that important, it is inevitable that many men will take the same attitude in their individual relationships. And the consequence, frequently, is woman abuse. Of course, not all men abuse women. Some are strong enough to turn their back on society's messages and to value their partners as equals. I am fortunate in enjoying a happy marriage with a kind and gentle man who not only supports me in my work but also willingly shares in the care of our daughter. But a frightening amount of men are unable to behave like that.

I have written this book to show women that they are

not alone, that what they are going through is part of a much wider scenario. And I am writing it in the hope that our society might acknowledge – and ultimately change – some of the subtle ways in which we give men permission to abuse women.

Because I talk to abused women almost every day of my life, I am using their stories to highlight the behaviour of their men. But – despite the fact that the immediate concern of refuges is to give the women a safe haven and emotional support – my overriding concern is to shift the spotlight from the women on to the men, and on to our society as a whole. A society which says, 'But he can't be abusive. He's so charming . . . '

1

Charm Syndrome Man

The Charm Syndrome is a pattern of behaviour. It is a man's use of charm to gain control over a woman. Once he has achieved that control, Charm Syndrome Man may or may not continue to charm his partner. But what he will always do is assert and reinforce his control by emotional and sometimes physical abuse.

When Melinda met Trevor, she was 'devastated' by his charm. 'He was very good-looking, highly intelligent. Very, very charming. I liked him a lot, we were very good companions, and he was fun to be with,' she told me. Eleven months later, after Melinda and Trevor had married and had had their first baby, he hit her for the first time. It was the beginning of a twelve-year nightmare which ended only in divorce.

Melinda is thirty-two, outgoing, bright, with a demanding and well-paid job in the city. Trevor is highly intelligent, a man who regretted not going to university after he left school. When he and Melinda met, she was more than happy to support him, so that he could become a mature student.

Melinda hardly fits the picture most people have of an abused woman as a careworn, pathetic creature, suffering at the hands of a husband who has one too many at the pub, then comes home and beats her in a drunken rage. Trevor only drank socially, and was the kind of guy that everyone liked. He was fun, good-looking, an entertaining conversationalist. 'He actually *liked* me, quite separately from everything else,' she says. 'He put me on a pedestal really. No one was allowed to swear in front of me, and as far as he was concerned, I was a real lady. He'd do all sorts of things for me – he used to hitchhike to London to see me and things like that. He made me feel special, unique really. He said that no other woman had made him feel so good, so loved. We were going to make a great team. He needed me, it was the two of us against the world.'

The men who abuse women may be dustbinmen, accountants, bus drivers or film producers. I have counselled women who have suffered terribly at the hands of policemen, clergymen and judges. On one occasion I was horrified to find myself counselling the wife of a lawyer who supported our work and was at that very time actually involved in proceedings on behalf of a battered wife, before going home to hit his own.

What these men have in common is that they are invariably the last people anyone would suspect of abusing their partners. They are the 'nice guys from next door' who are always willing to do a neighbour a favour: they will mend the plumbing, weed the garden, jump-start the car. They may be the men who seem to uphold strict moral standards, who are popular at parties or in the local pub. Or they may be quiet, 'steady' chaps, the ones 'you can always rely on'. Charm Syndrome Men present a likeable face to the rest of the world: charm obscures the abuser. And being liked feeds their self-image.

Some are intensely charismatic. The whole of America recently watched the trial of criminal lawyer Joel Steinberg, who had physically abused his lover Hedda Nussbaum so badly (on top of years of emotional abuse) that according to *Newsweek* magazine her face was distorted like 'a boxer's', and who was charged with the murder of their adopted daughter. Over six years he broke Hedda Nussbaum's knee and some ribs, choked her hard enough to damage her vocal chords, burned her body with a propane torch, knocked out her teeth, pulled out her hair, poked his fingers in her eyes and urinated on her.

In a court transcript, she told how she fell in love with Steinberg. 'I loved to listen to him,' she said. 'Basically, I worshipped him. He was the most wonderful man I had ever met. I believed he had supernatural, godlike power. He would praise me and build my ego. On the other hand, he was constantly critical. And he would strike me.'

The Charlotte Fedders case also hit the headlines, after her husband John – another lawyer – had admitted in court to having beaten his wife on several occasions during their eighteen-year marriage. The judge in the Fedders case said: 'When you put it all together, you have as classic a situation of cruelty . . . and a classic situation of excessively vicious conduct . . . as one can find.' John Fedders was the man about whom she had said when they first met, 'I knew he was the one love of my life.' In her book *Shattered Dreams* her co-author Laura Elliott talks of how Charlotte could hardly believe her luck that she had made such a catch. John, she says, was charming and witty – so romantic that he took her to see *The Sound of Music* and held her hand during the wedding scene. But before long the beatings began.

The irony is that he eventually won 25 per cent of the royalties from *Shattered Dreams*!

The men who abuse women may be glamorous and famous and there are countless examples of well-known actors, popstars and sportsmen who have admitted in court and elsewhere to physical abuse of their partners. One only has to read Tina Turner's book *I, Tina* for an example of how an apparently glamorous and exciting life can be a personal secret nightmare.

What is especially notable is that, whether their husbands are movie stars or lawyers or accounts clerks, in more or less the same breath as they describe their humiliation and pain, most abused women talk of the loving, caring, *charming* side of the men who abuse them. 'He could charm the birds out of the trees' is a phrase I hear over and over again. These women invariably remember the charming side of their partners, the side they fell in love with. They describe them as loving, tender, funny and considerate. More often than not, they explain that in between bouts of abuse their partners revert to being charmers. They can beg forgiveness, smother them in affection and promise they will never behave badly again. And because the women still care, they agree to give it just one more try . . .

▶ That word charm has cropped up again and again. At first it seemed astonishing, but soon – and repeatedly – I was making the connection between these two apparent opposites, charm and abuse, which seemed to run like two threads intertwined in the tapestry of these women's lives. It might be the charm of Dr Jekyll and the abuse of Mr Hyde – and, just as in Stevenson's novel, the activities of Mr Hyde are protected by the character of Dr Jekyll. ▲This is what I have come to call the Charm Syndrome.

Melinda is one of six women whose stories I have chosen to tell – because they are so typical. Let me introduce the others (naturally names and other details have been changed, to protect the identities of those involved).

Beverley is a twenty-eight-year-old fashion model, a stylish, attractive young woman who loves her work. The first time she met Dave, a singer who was performing in a nightclub, she remembers that 'He was totally charming, terribly well dressed, the perfect gentleman. He stood up on the stage and sang love songs looking into my eyes, and I fell for it. He seemed so together, very confident, but soft behind, very loving, very romantic. He'd take me out to dinner and let everyone know how he felt about me. He made me feel special.

'During the first six months we couldn't get enough of each other. No expense was spared. If we went on a picnic, he would have picked the most romantic spot, miles from anywhere, overlooking the sea. When we were mellow with vintage wine he would read me love poems. I couldn't believe my luck. He was so attentive. I never had to worry about a thing.

'I was in awe of him. He seemed such an amazing person. He knew about everything. He would always help me if there was anything I couldn't manage on my own. Our sex life was fantastic. He made everything seem so exciting. Even doing the shopping. In the supermarket queue he would whisper that he wanted to make love to me the moment we got back.'

Hazel is a twenty-four-year-old hairdresser. Her husband Jimmy is a builder. They met at a party. 'He could make you feel as though you were the only woman who had ever existed, he was so charming,' says Hazel. 'He would take me for long walks, and hold my hand. He was so attentive, as if his whole world was wrapped up in you. He could really charm the birds out of the trees.

'He had these great ideas, dreams really, about how he was going to build my ideal house for me. He'd sit for hours telling me the way he'd decorate it, where it would be, what the garden would be like . . . it all sounded so wonderful. It made me feel really important – he was going to do all these things just for me. I'd always wanted a lovely house and someone like Jimmy, so it was a bit like a dream come true.'

Rebecca was forty-six when she met Ralph, a solicitor. She had been widowed for several years and had three small children. Everyone thought of Ralph as a fine, upstanding man. He was ten years older than her, and had been married before, but he had been divorced for many years. He and Rebecca were introduced at a dinner party, discovered they shared a love of music and the theatre, and began to see each other regularly.

'When I thought of other men I had been out with,' says Rebecca, 'Ralph seemed perfect. Our mutual love of music brought us close together. We sang in a local choral society, which was a wonderful experience. We both loved walking, golf and tennis. He was very gentle and seemed to be fun-loving, on the spur of the moment suggesting outings to cafés, art galleries or concerts. He was extremely protective of me. He was very conscientious about his work as a solicitor and concerned about moral issues. I was impressed by that. He had such a strong sense of justice. He seemed so competent – you know, able to manage everything, yet at the same time so calm. I had never come across someone who provided such a sense of solidity. My friends, too, were won over by him. They thought he had real charm and told me how lucky I was.'

When Sally met Guy, she was a student at a polytechnic where he was a lecturer. 'I think I was bewitched by him,' she recalls. 'He was a very magnetic, educated, articulate man. I was studying for my finals, and he kept saying I'd work better if I took more time off to relax. He said, "Trust me. I'll look after you." And that is what I did, I suppose – trust him, I mean. And I did pass my finals. I can't think how, considering how much time I spent with him. He sort of took me over. We got completely wrapped up in each other. Before my exams he sent a telegram saying, "Good luck. I love you." He was wonderfully charming and I was flattered.'

Everyone thought that Laura and James had the perfect teenage romance. They met when he was at a public school and she was at an expensive girls' school. Both went to university but their relationship endured and when Laura was twenty-five they were married. 'He was a bright, witty, amusing person to be with,' says Laura. 'He was very attractive physically, everyone thought he was charming. We seemed to have a terrific relationship. I thought we were very lucky.'

I have met countless women either socially or in the course of my work, whose stories are astonishingly similar to those of these six women. The details and extent of abuse are different, yet invariably when I ask these women, 'What was he like when you first met?' the answer is the same. Each of these men, in his own way, is a charmer. Not just in the eyes of their partners, but in the eyes of many people they meet. Not only do they charm their partners, but they are able to get away with behaving abusively because unconsciously they use charm to convince everyone (including themselves) that they are great guys. After all, how could such terrific characters be abusers? This is vital to their self-image, which requires that they deny that they are abusers.

They may not all be witty, magnetic men, who can be extravagant in their affection. They may not all give red roses, buy champagne and quote Shakespeare. They may be 'rough diamonds': unsophisticated and inarticulate, or they may be quiet, undemonstrative types whose charm lies in their apparent solidity and dependability. But the common characteristic all these men share is their ability to make a woman feel special. To charm them. Many abusers, in fact, are womanisers.

Webster's dictionary defines charm as a 'magical power', associated with 'enchantment, spells and sorcery'. To charm someone, it explains, is to act on them with a 'compelling or magical force'. This is something completely different from being 'a nice guy', someone who is amusing and fun. Charm is, in fact, manipulative. To use charm is to influence, to bewitch someone, to bring them within your power. Ultimately to control them.

And that is the key word: *control*.

Of course it is possible for a man to be charming, to bewitch women, yet not to abuse them. The self-gratification he enjoys when a woman is besotted with him is often enough. But in the case of Charm Syndrome Man, he uses his charm to the ultimate, because it is *control* over his partner that he really wants. And he uses his charm to deceive others too.

My definition of woman abuse is this: systematic, patterned behaviour on the part of the abusive man, designed – consciously or subconsciously – to control and dominate 'his woman'. And in the armoury of the abuser, charm is both an essential weapon and a disguise . . .

2

A Pattern of Control

The first cracks in the charmer's make-up often begin to show once a woman has committed herself to him. One woman I helped told me that the violence began on her wedding night, when the man she had thought was 'so gorgeous, somebody to love me', slapped her for the first time.

Sally recalls the first time she was shocked by Guy's behaviour. 'We had been going to go out together on a Saturday, and he had to cancel it because he'd had to do an extra tutorial. After he'd gone, I was a bit bored so I rang up some girlfriends and we went bathing in the river. When Guy came home I told him, and he was furious that I had spent the day enjoying myself without him. He hardly spoke to me for days. I couldn't understand it. He had never behaved like that before and it threw me completely.'

The only time Laura recalls being confused at James's behaviour when they first started going out together was when she had gone to see a new play with some girlfriends, on a night when he was playing rugby. 'When he came home, I thought he'd be really interested to hear about the play,' she says, 'but instead he was really hurt that I had gone without him. He kept saying that that was the sort of special thing we should do together – and why hadn't I asked him to go. I had only gone on that night because I usually sat in while he played rugby. I felt so guilty at not putting him first, that I never did it again. Crazy, isn't it?'

It may be days, months or years before an abuser begins to wound his partner with blows or words, but whenever it begins it is devastating for the woman. What has happened to Mr Right? Where is the charmer, the man who can make a woman feel so loved, and appreciated, and special? And when the abuse begins after years, it is likely that it really began long before and that the woman simply failed to identify it.

Charm Syndrome Man begins to abuse when he feels he can take his partner for granted. Once he has persuaded the woman that he is the ideal man she has been searching for all her life, once she has committed herself to marriage or to a permanent relationship, Charm Syndrome Man no longer feels the need to charm her. He has used charm to control her for so long that she has become used to responding to his suggestions. Now he needs to charm her only in the moments when he fears he may be losing his control over her. For control is what a relationship is all about, as far as Charm Syndrome Man is concerned.

In my experience, women rarely have any way of knowing that they are embarking on life with an abusive man. By the time they find out, they are so embroiled in the relationship that it is very difficult to walk away. Looking back, some women recall 'niggles' early on in the relationship: perhaps an uncalled-for bout of jealousy, a temper tantrum or an unexpected verbal attack, but usually they dismiss it once their partner's good side reappears. Warning signals are written off as isolated incidents, because Charm Syndrome Man has an extraordinary ability to manipulate people, to cloak the controlling side of his nature with charm. As Sally explains: 'I think that I was rather dazed by the sudden changes in Guy's behaviour, but because things went back to normal pretty quickly, and he would be loving and considerate until the next incident, I didn't let it bother me too much.'

An abusive man may use a whole range of weapons to control his partner, from actual physical abuse to verbal, emotional, psychological, sexual or social abuse.

Remember, non-physical forms of abuse are as potent in destroying a woman's confidence and personality as violence, though they may be less obvious. An abuser can cripple his partner emotionally by humiliating and degrading her, just as surely as he can wound her with blows.

And always, just when he senses that she may be on the point of walking out, Charm Syndrome Man resorts to his greatest weapon: charm. He may say he is sorry, tell her he loves her, that he hates himself for acting the way he did, it was only because he was under stress, or had had too much to drink, that it will never happen again . . . that he needs her support more than ever. 'After all we've been through, how can you throw away the most important relationship you've ever had?' is a typical plea. Charm Syndrome Man uses charm to confuse his partner, to make her forget the bad times and bind her to him further. As one woman, looking back on her relationship, described it: 'It is like being a fish on a hook.'

In the following sections I shall look at the ways in which Charm Syndrome Man controls his partner. There is no definitive checklist of abuse, nothing to say that a man is necessarily abusive because he is possessive, jealous, tight with money or prefers his wife to stay at home rather than work. A woman needs to look at every area of her relationship and see if there is a pattern. Ultimately, she needs to ask herself whether or not she is in control of her own life, or whether it is her partner who pulls the strings.

If a woman is afraid to be herself, or avoids doing certain things because she is afraid of her partner's reaction; if he prevents her from acting the way she wants to, or makes her do things against her will, by using physical force, verbal abuse, threats or bullying, or if he confuses her by treating her contemptuously one moment and lovingly the next, then she is being abused. All the more so if she *feels* she is being abused.

'He Always Had to Be the Boss'

'We were playing a game of Monopoly,' says Beverley, the fashion model, 'and in the middle of the game, Dave stood up, tipped the board upside down and accused me of cheating, then he stormed out of the place. And I said: "My God, it's only a game." But as the relationship went on, it was as if he had to win at everything – that was really important. He had to prove to himself all the time that he was better than me and he took great delight in putting me down in front of everyone.'

In his bid for control, an abusive man tries to dominate every aspect of his partner's life. He may telephone constantly – whether his partner is at home or work – to check up on what she is doing, using the flimsiest of excuses, such as 'Can you buy a roll of Sellotape for my desk?' or 'Don't forget to pick up the dry cleaning.' He constantly has to prove he is boss even over the tiniest details, such as the clothes his partner wears, or which programme to watch on the television. In one headline-hitting case a man actually killed his wife for putting the mustard pot in the 'wrong' place on the table.

After Rebecca and Ralph, the solicitor, were married, she began to notice that he made more and more of the decisions. She told me, 'If I was really interested in watching a nature documentary, he would insist on watching *The Professionals*. I knew it was useless to express any interest in a programme. Then when *he* had had enough TV for the evening, he would go over and switch off, then rip the plug out of the wall, leave the room and turn off the light, leaving me in darkness, as though I didn't even exist. But if I wanted to go to bed early and read a book, there was no question of it. I had to sit up and watch the late news with him.

'When I was on the phone, he would come along and shout, "Goodbye!" to make me hang up. Then if I still carried on the conversation, he would just come over and press the button to cut me off, gloating while he did it.

'I know it all sounds so unimportant, but it built up to be so incredibly oppressive. Once he drove me so mad I went out into the night – it was in the middle of winter and it was snowing, but I was furious and I couldn't care less. I just wanted to get out of that oppressive atmosphere.

'I could never suggest we go out. It always had to be his idea. And if we did go anywhere, and I was frantically trying to get the children dressed, Ralph would go out and sit in the car and hoot the horn aggressively to hurry me up. If for some reason he had forgotten something and had to go back into the house, that was a different matter.'

An abusive man often has clear rules about the space in the house: if there is a spare room he will commandeer it for his study, in which he cannot be disturbed. His possessions must not be moved or touched by anyone.

Ralph had his own bathroom. 'Nobody else was allowed in it,' Rebecca says. 'His excuse was that he had to get to work on time, but he still didn't allow anyone to use it at the weekends. He was absolutely obsessive about everything. Everything had to be in the right place. The children's toys had to be put away before he came home.'

Ralph made his point about who was boss in petty ways. On one occasion when she had just cooked dinner, Rebecca says, 'I was walking from the kitchen to the table with a heavy casserole, to put it on the table, and Ralph was standing in my way. Now, I am sure if you did this and your husband was standing there he would move without a word, but Ralph didn't move out of the way and I was nearly dropping the casserole. It was red hot. I said, "Come on, Ralph, let me put it down," and he said, "Walk around me." And from then on his attitude was "*I am me* and you must not encroach on my territory."'

Guy insisted that Sally keep her books upstairs, while *his* should be on display downstairs. 'His books were more important, more intellectual. And there were so many other things,' says Sally. 'For instance, he had his desk in the living room, where the television and stereo were, but I felt I couldn't go in there while he was working. I couldn't play his records, because I'd scratch them, and I couldn't play mine because he said they weren't in good enough condition and they would damage his stylus. When I was watching television with a friend once, he came in and started to chip the paint off a metal cupboard he wanted to repaint. It made screeching noises, like fingernails on a blackboard, but at first I tried to ignore it, rather than start a row. When it was really driving me crazy, and I asked him to stop, he just gave me a long hard stare – he had these really penetrating dark-brown eyes – and carried on chipping.

'There was no escaping him even when he was away. He expected me to come home straight away after work to let his dog out, and after that it wasn't worth driving all the way back into town. I realise now that I hadn't got a life of my own. Even when he was out of the house I felt him as a heavy presence.'

An abuser has rigid ideas about the roles of men and women: men make the rules, and women obey them. Women, he believes, are emotional and incapable of rational thought – unlike men. That men are rational, women intuitive, is a distinction taught by a man-dominated society: irrational, emotional women cannot be trusted with decision-taking. Their role is in the background. So, in an abuser's view, the very fact of being a man gives him certain privileges. He believes that the woman's place is to stay at home with the children, so that *he* can go out. Jimmy the builder was a case in point. After he and Hazel were married there were no more romantic walks in the park. 'He was more interested in his mates than in me,' she says. Soon after the wedding she became pregnant and, once the baby was born, he was out more than ever. 'He would never ever say: "I must get home to Hazel and the baby," he would say, "I'm the master of the house. If I want to stay out all night long drinking I can." He had to be the master, he had to be the boss and he had to let everybody else know it.

'He was always going out, and on one occasion I

thought, "It's my turn," so I asked him if I could go, and
he said okay. When I was about to leave, he knocked me
all around the kitchen, saying, "Where do you think you're
going then?" He insisted that I had to stay in because *he'd*
made arrangements with a friend – I later discovered the
"friend" was a barmaid in the pub around the corner, and
everyone knew what was going on, apart from me.

'I was so frightened, I ran round to my mother's house for
help, but she's a really strong Catholic, and her attitude is
that marriage is sacred, and you have to work at it. She kept
telling me that I had to be forgiving and try harder to make it
work. She said that her life hadn't been a bed of roses either,
and that women can't expect to have perfect marriages. I
think if I'd had somebody to encourage me at that point, I
would have packed my bags and left, but the very person
I thought would support me was saying, "Go back and try
harder." It just made me feel even more alone.'

Often the incidents over which Charm Syndrome Man
makes such a fuss seem quite trivial, and it is invariably
easier for a woman to go along with her partner's wishes,
just to keep the peace – but after a while this constant
interference in her life, and the strain of forever trying to
anticipate his needs in order to prevent physical or verbal
abuse, can become oppressive and debilitating.

Guy made Sally's life hell by trying to dominate the
decision-making. She says, 'I can remember one time
when we were deciding how to decorate our first flat.
We had a row about what colour to do it in and he got
really angry. It wasn't a case of just having a difference
of opinion over colours – I was expecting that – but he
just started screaming, "You stupid bitch!" I was shocked
and hurt. He made me feel so small. But I thought it wasn't
worth the aggravation, so I gave in and painted the wall a
bright yellow – horrible!' she laughs. 'He didn't help at all.
He only seemed interested in winning the battle.

'I can think of something else, although to an outsider
it might seem trivial, but in actual fact he was being
unreasonable. I used to love cooking fantastic meals and

he used to love eating them. He actively encouraged me and bragged about my culinary skills to his friends. So of course I went out of my way to please him even more, spending my grant money on expensive ingredients. Then suddenly he would accusingly tell me that he had put on weight because of my cooking . . . so I would prepare less fattening food for a while only to be criticised for not bothering. I couldn't win.

'I was willing to put up with his idiosyncrasies partly because I thought that is the price you pay for living with a genius, and also because I was sure that every relationship had its ups and downs. After all, most of the time he was wonderfully charming and romantic and everyone liked him.'

Guy changed so easily from charmer to boor that Sally was constantly 'walking on eggshells', never sure when the tiniest thing would spark off a torrent of abuse. 'Over time', she says, 'his behaviour became more and more unpredictable. I never knew what would upset him next.'

'In the beginning he had encouraged me to talk about my work. But after we'd been living together for a while, if I started to discuss it with him, he would tap his watch, sigh, turn eyes to the ceiling and tell me my time was up. At other times he would seen genuinely interested and encourage me to talk, and then after some time he would stop me dead and say I had gone over the time limit. It was so humiliating and infuriating, but I never challenged him.

'He was very precise about time. He used to get really upset if I was late, even a few minutes. Once I had invited a girlfriend I hadn't seen for years to stop by and have tea, and also meet Guy for the first time. I thought I would stop off at the bakery on my way home to buy something nice for the occasion.

'I was *six* minutes late. When I said hello Guy just glared at me. I couldn't imagine what I had done wrong. He was angry that I was late – a whole six minutes – and demanded a detailed account of where I had been during the six minutes. When my girlfriend arrived he went into the bedroom and refused to come out. She thought it was all very strange, especially as she had come over partly to meet him. I was so embarrassed, but even those feelings had to be suppressed. Later he spent hours telling me that he wouldn't have behaved that way if I hadn't been late. In the end I felt responsible for the whole thing and wound up apologising to *him!*'

Guy, in true Charm Syndrome fashion, could never accept that he was less than perfect. Nothing could be wrong with *his* behaviour – Sally must have forced him to act that way. Sally told me many similar stories, but, like most abused women, she didn't link them in any way. It takes time to realise just how easily an abusive man can manipulate his partner into believing that everything is *her* fault, not *his*. Similarly, it takes time to realise that the relationship is abusive. Some women think the abuse is just a passing phase – after all, as Sally remarked, every relationship has its ups and downs.

Hazel's husband Jimmy also had to have his way over every little detail. She told me, 'He had to have everything just right. I never had time to think what I wanted. I always had to do everything to make him happy, like keeping the baby quiet. If we went out I had to look happy or I'd get a hiding when I got home. People might have thought I *was* happy, but he was pulling the strings. If it was a toss-up between using money to buy food or him going for a drink, it had to go on drink. If I disagreed with something, anything he wanted, and I wouldn't go along with, I got a hiding.'

Abusive men are frequently fanatical about the most trivial things. 'Guy was always very precise,' says Sally. 'Our spontaneous, exotic gourmet dinners turned into a kind of competition. Romantic moments were spoiled when he would measure our wine glasses to make sure I didn't have more than him. Towards the end of the relationship I used to practically fill his glass right up to the edge. As soon as he had a sip I would fill his glass up again.'

When Rebecca first met Ralph, she was impressed by the fact that 'he seemed so competent – you know, able to manage everything. He was extremely reliable.' When he phoned her every day to say what time he would arrive home from the office, she took it as a sign of his consideration. She soon realised that it was his way of signalling what time he wanted his dinner on the table – and if it wasn't ready he would create an atmosphere for the rest of the evening. It was also a ploy on his behalf to make sure she stayed in in the evenings, to wait for his call.

'When we first lived in the country we had just one car and I used to drive Ralph the twelve miles to the station and then drive home again,' says Rebecca. 'I had to wait for him to call from the office every night between five-forty and seven-fifteen. He would tell me which train he would catch, what time it left Victoria and what time it would arrive at our local station. This meant that if anyone else phoned up during the time he wanted to call, I would have to be quite short with them, because Ralph would be furious if he rang up and the line was engaged.

'I felt I had to comply with his demands because I didn't work (no wife of his was going to work for a living!), therefore he held the purse strings and the least I could do was ferry him back and forth to the station, so he could bring home the money.

'Even when we had two cars I was amazed to find that he still insisted on this arrangement rather than leaving one of the cars at the station all day. I can see now that it was part of the control scenario. At the time I was willing to go along with it – I was a complete puppet – but I did find it all an enormous strain, especially with three lively children to care for. After a day of freedom from his rigid rules we suddenly all had to rush around putting everything back in exactly the right place and making out that nothing had moved all day long.

'Strangely enough I grew to appreciate his telephone calls as warning signals. They gave us time to psyche ourselves up for his homecoming.'

Laughingly Rebecca admits, 'One of the things which irritated me most was that he would never let me sit on the edge of the sofa. He said it ruined it – so I used to take great delight in walking all over the sofa when he was out! Just for the hell of it!'

'He Was Jealous of Everything and Everybody'

Like many women who believe they have found the perfect partner, Beverley was shocked the first time Dave flew into a jealous rage, but she dismissed it as an isolated incident. 'It was only three months after we got together. Our relationship couldn't have been better, and by that time he'd asked me to marry him,' she recalls. 'We were at his family home. His parents had gone away on holiday and I was just wearing a dressing-gown of his. Some man was mentioned, I can't remember what was said, but I just remember that he spat at me, spat at my face, and then pushed me against a wall, which ripped this dressing-gown – which I came to realise later was absolutely nothing! I was hysterical. I was absolutely frightened to death and ran out of the house.

'I couldn't believe it, I was going to marry this man, and I couldn't believe it wasn't going to work. I thought it was just an outburst. I didn't realise there would be more and worse. Apparently I slept with everybody – which I didn't do, and wouldn't do either, because I'm a very monogamous person, a fact which Dave would never believe.'

The very possibility, however imaginary, that his partner might be unfaithful to him assumes enormous proportions in the mind of Charm Syndrome Man, because it threatens to dilute his control over her. Not only that, but he risks being ridiculed by the outside world as 'less than a real man', because he cannot keep his own wife in line. Her past boyfriends, current friends, the children, even inanimate objects she treasures, appear to him as threats. He is jealous of her job, particularly if she is more successful than he is, and suspicious of her colleagues. He may try to entice her to work in the same place as him, suggesting that he hates to be apart from her, or it is another area of their life they can share. His real motive is that he wants to keep an eye on her.

An abuser's fears are almost always totally unfounded. Melinda told me, 'I am the most faithful person in the world, I couldn't have been more faithful – it is anathema to me to have affairs or anything like that. And I never looked at anybody else, it just didn't occur to me, and somewhere he knew that.'

However, many abusers constantly imagine that their partners have lovers, becoming so suspicious that they subject them to hours of interrogation and accusation. Ironically, for most abused women, an affair is the last thing on their minds. Invariably they have been brought up to believe in fidelity and, besides, they are either too frightened of the consequences of being found out, or they have come to think that all men are abusive, so why should they leave the frying pan for the fire? Even so, women often tell me that they end up confessing to things they haven't done, just to be left alone. They may be beaten as a result, but at least the harassment stops for a while.

An abuser also uses jealousy as a weapon to isolate his partner: if seeing friends and family (of either sex), keeping in touch with previous boyfriends and husbands, or even talking to other men causes him to create such a storm of physical or verbal abuse, it is easier for the woman to avoid outside contact. Once again, she is changing and moulding her behaviour in an attempt to keep the peace. And because his jealousy isolates her, she becomes more dependent on him to answer all her emotional needs, and less able to talk to people who can give her another viewpoint on her predicament. The result is that he is able to control her even more.

Most of us have experienced some sort of pangs of jealousy at one time or another, and even in the healthiest of relationships there are sometimes moments when a man or woman feels put out and hurt because their partner has spent all night at a party flirting with someone else. Usually in the cold light of day, after a few cross words, all is forgiven and forgotten.

When a woman lives with an abusive man, however, the situation is different. It is a myth, perpetuated by the abuser, that his jealousy is a sign of his love for his girlfriend or wife. Though at first his jealous outbursts may seem like isolated incidents, they become more and more frequent and unfounded. In an abusive man, jealousy is about control.

An abusive man, albeit subconsciously, uses jealousy to keep his partner 'in her place'. Because his outbursts are unpredictable, she 'walks on eggshells', in fear of him; she is careful not to mention old boyfriends or that her boss took her out to lunch. Even close girlfriends pose a threat. So she becomes wary and secretive.

An abuser also makes his partner feel guilty. He will frequently accuse her of dressing too provocatively, or smiling too invitingly: the implication is that she is a slut, who is just dying to have an affair with any man she meets. Hazel says, 'If we went out anywhere, when we came home the first thing Jimmy would say was: "You made a bloomin' fool of me. I saw you making eyes at such and such a bloke," and I wouldn't know what on earth he was talking about.

'When we went out together, my eyes couldn't leave his face. If my eyes looked one way, he'd accuse me of looking at a man. There was an Australian barman at our local pub, and I used to like talking to him because he had this lovely drawl – I didn't fancy him, but Jimmy really pulled me up on it. He said, "Imagining yourself having it off with him, are you?" You know, he was just stupid, really daft. I mean I wouldn't have dreamed of having an affair anyway. It didn't enter my head.'

Charm Syndrome Man is completely irrational in his jealousy: everyone from the postman to his partner's boss at work comes under suspicion, if they threaten to dilute his control over her. One man even stopped his wife from bouncing her four-year-old on her knee – because he was jealous of her spending her affection on him.

An abuser will try to turn his partner against her friends and colleagues by putting them down, or pitting them against each other. Melinda remembers that Trevor was so jealous of her work and her colleagues, even though she had earned enough to put him through university, that he tried to turn her against them by implying that her boss was giving one of her colleagues (a good friend) all the best jobs; although she did not really believe it, it was enough to sow seeds of doubt and make her feel uneasy. 'I had to work,' she says, 'but it was a sort of Catch 22, because the more successful I became, the more insecure he became, and the harder he made it for me.'

On one occasion, he revealed his jealousy in a quite different way, after she had been to the Christmas party given by the firm where she worked. His resentment was compounded by the fact that there were only five women invited to the function, and 1500 men. 'It was an honour to be asked,' says Melinda. 'I bought a new dress, and a week before I told him, "I have to go to this thing and I will be home by quarter to twelve." He was in Guildford that night, he'd been away doing research for his course, and the babysitter said the phone kept on ringing from quarter to twelve. Every five minutes he would ring and say, "Is she back?"

'I got back about quarter-past twelve and the girl said the last phone call had been about five minutes before I walked in. The babysitter left, and I went to bed, because I was very tired. The next thing I knew I was being punched. When Trevor found I wasn't home, he had got into the car, and driven down from Guildford to London at ten past midnight, and he went completely berserk. He punched my face – he'd always been very careful not to hit me where it showed before – he hit my head, and I was unrecognisable the next day. And then the children woke up (we had two by now) and it was my daughter who stopped him – by that time he had pushed me down the stairs and I was unconscious on the floor. She just screamed at him to stop and he just stopped. And I came round and said to her, "Go and get your brother, get him out of the house and go next door." And then I got out too. I had said that if he hit me one more time, I was going. And so that was it. I never lived with him again.'

Rebecca enrolled at an evening class one night a week – ironically she did so because once they were married this 'amazing man' who 'knew about everything' frequently humiliated her by calling her ignorant. 'One night,' she told me, 'he came to meet me and was in a terrible state. He pushed me into the car and shouted at me all the way home. When we got in, he accused me of having an affair with the teacher and insisted that I was never to go to college again. He kept on at me until four o'clock in the morning and then finally went to sleep, leaving me thinking I really had done something wrong.

'I found out later that he was having an affair with a girl at work – it took me years to get over that. I wanted to leave him then and there, when I found out, but he begged me to forgive him, and he behaved so kindly and reasonably for a while. And there were the children to think of.'

Rebecca's husband, like many abusive men, operated a double standard. He was jealous of her every move, yet it was perfectly okay for *him* to have affairs because that fitted his male image. As Del Martin observes in *Battered Wives*, the unfaithful man 'has been portrayed as a player of the game. A husband is encouraged to develop his extra-marital style to such a degree that, in our day and age, he is considered somewhat ridiculous for remaining faithful to his wife. It might even be said that in certain circles the only thing more ridiculous than a faithful husband is a cuckolded one. . . . '

If an abuser is actually being unfaithful himself, he

will often try to transfer the guilt by accusing his wife of doing the same thing. However ridiculous the accusation may be, it serves as a smokescreen for his own infidelities. And, after all, why should he feel guilty if she is behaving in the same way? Furthermore, since an abuser thinks of his wife as a possession, he may even be subconsciously lining up a new woman to control, should his present relationship fail.

Charm Syndrome Man is very often a womaniser. Sally suspected that Guy was having affairs, but he told her she was paranoid for thinking any such thing. Yet she later found out that he belonged to a dating club. Laura suffered even more directly as a result of James's affairs. Like many women, whose partners are being unfaithful, she recalls finding out she had a mysterious vaginal infection. 'This is a great joke,' she says. 'I mean, I laugh about this like crazy now, because I remember going to the doctor, and she was saying, "Look. Do you understand that this is sexually transmitted?" and I was saying, "Yes." And she was saying, "Er, what I'm trying to say to you is, either you or your partner has acquired this from somebody else, and both of you have got to take treatment."

'I came home knowing I hadn't been with someone else,' says Laura, yet when she confronted James, suggesting he was having an affair, 'He said, "Nonsense, nonsense, absolute rubbish." And I believed it! But I think you get so worn down that you are prepared to believe just about everything. And yet somewhere you know it's not quite right. He'd had affairs pretty well constantly, though I hadn't known about them at the time.'

Charm Syndrome Man is dependent on his partner, but this often goes unnoticed because he appears so self-assured and because he is so good at controlling his relationships. In reality, his frail self-image requires an adoring woman, and often one such woman is not enough: he may have a steady partner and a stream of disposable mistresses.

Past husbands or boyfriends are just as much a threat

to Charm Syndrome Man as imaginary rivals – as Beverley discovered all too soon. 'Dave used to ask me how many lovers I'd had and say, "Oh, I bet you've had loads," and talk about thirty or forty – unbelievable numbers,' she says. 'He would ask me for figures and I'd say five, or whatever. I said I wasn't really involved with any of them, but this was just as bad as if I had said that I was madly in love with them all. I mean you couldn't win.

'During certain periods, he would wake me up in the morning and say, "Well, what about So-and-So? Did you enjoy it with him? You did, didn't you?" and I would say, "No, I didn't," and he would say, "Are you sure?" And that would happen every morning, with outbursts during the day – not necessarily hitting me, though sometimes he'd slap me across the face and bruise my ribs.'

Dave controlled and confused Beverley by punctuating the abuse with tenderness, begging to be forgiven, telling her he only acted the way he did because he loved her. 'Once it had settled down, those spaces between big instances like black eyes were good – I counted three weeks once when he didn't do anything. That was the record,' she says. 'And that's partly why I stayed. I mean he only cared about these men, ha-ha, because he "loved me so much". He always counteracted with that.'

Sally recalls, 'One day when we were out with my brother and sister-in-law, Guy was filling his car up with petrol and suddenly discovered he didn't have his wallet with him. So I got my bag and wrote out a cheque. The man at the petrol station asked for my address on the back of the cheque (it was in the days before cheque cards) and I automatically put the telephone number too. Then Guy refused to drive out of the station until I explained my actions. He was convinced I fancied the attendant – who was at least forty years older than me – because I had written down my phone number.

'He insisted on an explanation in front of my brother and his wife and demanded I get the cheque back and write out a new one. After several tense minutes he drove off in a huff and refused to speak to any of us for the rest of the day, even throughout supper.'

Abusive men never forget incidents such as these. They will bring them up again and again over the years, whenever they need to reinforce their current bout of jealousy.

Guy was even jealous of Sally's parents, who wrote to tell her they were coming over to England from their home in New Zealand on a business trip. 'My mum was desperate to see me after three years,' she says. 'After London, they were going on to see some cousins in Jersey for a week, and they wanted me to join them. Guy was outraged at the suggestion that I should abandon him for a whole week. He kept this up for months before the actual event. Believe it or not, he managed to make me feel guilty and his attitude spoiled my reunion with my parents.

'Because I was doing something which he felt excluded him, he got angry over the most stupid things. On the way to the airport to meet my parents, we stopped at our favourite pub for a snack, and – I know it sounds silly – I ordered a salmon and cucumber sandwich, which cost seventy-nine pence. He was so angry and sarcastic about the price. He kept saying, "You always have to have the most extravagant thing! Why can't you have cheese like everybody else?"

'It was all so ridiculous, but at the time I felt so depressed. I was really looking forward to seeing my parents, and he kept putting a dampener on it all. He went on and on about that sandwich all the way to the airport, and even after they had gone home to New Zealand he brought it up again. . . . I realised later it wasn't about the money, it was his way of punishing me, of showing me how angry he was that I had put someone else in front of him.

'Even when I went to Jersey, he phoned every few hours, and if I was out he wanted to know exactly where I had been, and who I had been talking to. He made it all seem very romantic – he couldn't bear me to be away, he cared about me so much that he had to make sure I was okay – but I can see now that he was just checking up on me. Not only was he jealous of my family, but I'm sure he was convinced that I was going to run off with someone else the moment I was away from him.'

Many women tell me their husbands and boyfriends are jealous of their relationships with members of their family. 'He said he wanted me to himself, he didn't want anybody else to have me' is the kind of comment I hear so often. Abusive men are also frequently jealous of their own children, because they divert their partners' attention. This may be one reason why so many men attack their wives during pregnancy. And over and over again I hear stories from women whose husbands refused to attend the birth of their children. Often they also overreact when their wives are breastfeeding children. This kind of jealousy is not uncommon even in non-abusive relationships, if a man feels ignored in favour of the new arrival. But abusive men go much further, making their partners feel guilty because they have chosen to breastfeed. Some women actually give up breastfeeding because of their partners' attitudes.

Laura's husband James first sexually abused her during the period in which she was breastfeeding her daughter, as if to remind her that *he* should be the centre of her attention. Laura remembers, 'The abuse got worse as the children came along. He felt more and more out of it, or whatever. It certainly got worse then. He always had to centre on *me*. The kids always got shoved to one side. When they were a bit older, he'd tell them to get out of the room, he was talking to me. That really used to hurt me.' She recalled a time when James refused to let her go and watch the children in their nursery-school nativity play. He had refused to go, because he wanted to watch a documentary on the television, and he insisted she should stay with *him* rather than be with the children.

Another woman I met told how her husband was so jealous he even accused her of having sex with her nine-year-old son, a suspicion which totally disgusted her.

Some abusers are even jealous of objects, if they seem to threaten their monopoly over their partners' affections. Hazel's husband Jimmy noted anything she particularly loved. 'In the next dispute,' she says, 'it would be destroyed. For instance I love sewing and one day I said to someone in his presence, "I love my sewing machine." Some time afterwards when he was in a childlike temper, he picked it up above his head and slammed it to the floor, and of course it broke. It was as if he was jealous of an inanimate object.'

'He Always Put Me Down'

Guy never missed an opportunity to undermine Sally's self-confidence and make her feel inadequate. He nagged her, constantly picking up on anything he could interpret as a fault in her character, gradually eroding her sense of self-esteem. 'It was almost as if he was on the lookout for flaws in my character,' says Sally. 'He would pick up on the most trivial things.

'For example, one day I gave my mother a quick ring to see how she was getting on. Guy was peeling potatoes for supper and listening to *The Archers*, so I went into the hall to phone. When I finished the conversation, I went back into the kitchen, to be greeted by Guy saying disapprovingly, "Do you realise you just said 'okay' *fourteen* times?" I sensed that his motives for saying this were negative, but I couldn't work out why he did it. I felt really embarrassed, humiliated and so ashamed, and then before I knew it I was promising to watch my "okays" in future.'

Taken as an isolated incident, it seems very trivial, yet by this stage of their relationship Sally was exhausted by Guy's constant need to put her down. His unceasing criticism of the way she looked and behaved and thought wore her down like water dripping on a stone. Not only did he criticise her, but he was continually disparaging about her friends and colleagues at work, even her intelligence.

This endless undermining of her personality kept him firmly in control. Sally began to be more and more submissive, doubting her own opinions and relying on his.

Many women suffer such acute humiliation, degradation and bewilderment at the hands of their abusers that their self-esteem takes a severe battering. Instead of seeing themselves as worthwhile, important and valid people, they feel inferior, because their personality has been consistently mocked and attacked. They feel unattractive, usually because their partners have told them they are. They feel worthless, unwanted, insecure; they doubt their ability to make relationships work; they are unsure of their judgement and continually apologise for their actions. They say, 'If only I hadn't done this,' or 'I wish I were different.'

Many of the abused women I talk to are highly intelligent, respected, professional people, who are perfectly capable of trusting their own judgement and making decisions at high levels, yet in their personal relationships these same women often feel nervous and unsure of themselves as a direct effect of their partner's controlling behaviour. It is hard enough for women to have high self-esteem anyway in a male-dominant world. Many women already feel vulnerable – and when women are abused as well, they feel doubly worthless and insecure. To have self-esteem you need to feel in control of your life.

Trevor would constantly tell Melinda that she was 'hopeless'. 'He'd say, "When you met me, you thought you were somebody special, didn't you? I bet you don't now, do you?" and I used to say, "No." I think I underestimated the power of the verbal and emotional abuse at the time, the things he used to say to me. He'd call me slag, whore, bitch, dog – you name it, very denigrating names,' she says.

Hazel, too, says, 'Jimmy used to call me slag, trollop, horrible things, because he knew it upset me, that it was the one thing I couldn't get hardened to.' Hazel had been brought up in a warm, happy family and made friends easily, yet by the time she left Jimmy, she felt so physically bruised, psychologically scarred and sexually humiliated that, she told me, 'I felt no one would want me after what he had put me through. He destroyed all my self-confidence. He told me nobody liked me, that people only put up with me because I was with him – you know, that I lived in his shadow. I felt drained, just drained. As if I was nothing, as if I was worthless.'

'You're no good for anyone' is the kind of put-down women report to me time and time again. Laura told me that, in one sickening telephone call after they had split up, James had snarled at her, 'I dragged you up out of the gutter. Why don't you do everyone a favour and go and kill yourself?' Then he hung up.

One woman I spoke to told me that her husband frequently acted as if she did not even exist. In one such instance, she had spent all day painting and decorating their home, not even stopping to have anything to eat. When her husband came back from work that evening, having stopped to have a drink with colleagues on the way, he brought in a takeaway kebab for himself – and nothing for her, despite the fact that he knew she would not have had dinner without him. Like most women who recount such stories, she was embarrassed at the triviality of it, yet this was only one example amid numerous others which had left her feeling hurt that she had sunk so far in her husband's estimation that he barely even acknowledged her existence.

This woman's husband also attacked her self-confidence by being cruel about her appearance. She had a scar on her neck from a growth which had been removed when she was ten. 'People say they don't notice it, but I know it's there,' she says, 'and my husband knew I had a really bad inferiority complex about it. When I first met him he would say, "Oh I don't notice," but later he would say things like "When I first saw your scar it made me want to be sick."'

Hazel knew what it was like to have her appearance constantly criticised. 'Apart from telling me that I was useless at everything, that I was no good,' she says, 'Jimmy

used to say that I was fat and horrible, that I was lucky to
have him as nobody else would look at me. After a while
I really started to believe it. I stopped caring about what I
looked like, basically because what was the point? I never
went anywhere and I never saw anyone. The only person
I saw was him, and if I did make the effort and try to look
nice, put a bit of make-up on or something, he'd say, "What
the hell are you all dressed up for? Who have you had round
here?"'

Dave used terror tactics to humiliate and frighten
Beverley in order to undermine her personality. One day,
she told me, 'He came home and he came up to me and
said, "Do you love me?" and I said "Yes," and I went to put
my arms around him, and he thumped me in the stomach
and just kept hitting and kicking me, kicking and hitting.
He hadn't done that before. I was just thinking, "My God,
this is it, he really is going to kill me now – what can I do?"

'We were in a top-floor flat so I couldn't get outside,
and he dragged me right across the flat by my hair into the
kitchen, then he got out the kitchen knife, and I thought,
"Oh, *no!*" Even though I thought he might not mean to kill
me, it is very easy to kill somebody with a blade like that
and he was angry.

'I kept yelling, "*I love you! I love you!*" as if that was
the answer and that would stop him. And I put out my
hands and got my fingers cut – but do you know what
he was doing? He was cutting my hair off! My hair came
down to my waist, and he cut it all off. And then he just
sat there saying, "You're ugly now." Because, you see, he
didn't want me to be attractive, and he hacked my hair off
so that it was one inch long. You don't realise how easily
hair comes off with a sharp knife – just two cuts and that
was it.

'Every time I saw myself in the mirror I looked so ugly, I
felt this great sense of despair. I felt worthless, that I must
be a really bad person to make him do this to me.'

By deliberately damaging Beverley's self-esteem, Dave
could make himself feel superior to her, and therefore

more entitled to be in control. Ironically, though, the hair-cutting incident drove Beverley away. 'Despite the sense of humiliation, I had enough strength to leave,' she says. 'I knew the situation was beyond my control.'

An abuser will often use social abuse to undermine his partner, humiliating her in front of friends and family, often in subtle ways. As one woman explained, 'When my husband's sister and her boyfriend came to visit, he brought them in a cup of tea and cakes and biscuits, but he left me out. He didn't give me a cup and he never offered me a cake.'

Laura told me that James would make her feel she had behaved foolishly in front of his friends. 'I would be blamed for having said the wrong thing, which to me wouldn't have seemed like the wrong thing in any way. He would say I had put my foot in it over something which I didn't think was justified at all. He made me feel small and insignificant. He liked to put me down in front of other people, sort of saying, "What on earth is that you're wearing?" and "You don't know what you are talking about" and "You don't understand." Anything to make me feel small.'

The point about this sort of social abuse is that an abuser is always in control, unlike his partner, who never knows how he will behave towards her in front of other people.

Trevor would always pick an argument or try to degrade Melinda, just before she went off to an important meeting. 'He would find some excuse to put me down, to upset me, to be aggressive and abusive so I would always arrive feeling very unsure of myself, very insecure and very, very weak,' she remembers. 'I would be needing to communicate with people in a position of responsibility, with a lot to express, and all I would feel like doing was sitting down and crying. It was such a horrible feeling, it actually prevented me from communicating with other people, and communicating about my work.'

Jimmy, like many abusive men, undermined Hazel in another, very powerful way: he attacked her role as a mother. 'He'd say, "You're bringing up our son all wrong,"' she says. '"He's soft, he's pathetic." I suppose deep down I knew it was a game that he was playing with me, and nothing to do with my son, or anything I did with him. But he made me feel as if I was a failure at my marriage and I wasn't a good mother – as if I wasn't a good woman, I suppose.'

James tried to control Laura by undermining her role as mother, even after they had separated. He went so far as actually to ring up her children's school, saying, 'Laura's mad, she's drunk, she's taking drugs, she's not a reasonable mother. She's an alcoholic and a whore.' Another time, he promised to pay the school fees; not only did he fail to pay them, but, says Laura, 'He told the bursar he'd given me the money and I'd spent it. It was a new school and they didn't know me. The bursar rang me up and said, "I'm sorry your daughters can't come back to school. I've been told you've got the money and you haven't paid the bill." And I said, "It's not true, I haven't got it." He said, "Well, look, I'm awfully sorry, but I can't enter into that sort of thing," and of course he couldn't. I mean it's no good saying, "It's not true," is it?'

'I Thought I Must Be Going Crazy'

Melinda felt so manipulated, confused and disorientated by her husband's abusive behaviour that she compared him to the husband in the film *Gaslight*. 'I felt he was trying to convince me that I was insane,' she says.

The film *Gaslight* starred Ingrid Bergman, with Charles Boyer as the husband who seemed so romantic and charming, while all the time he was manipulating his wife into thinking she was going crazy. His technique was to hide jewellery, then accuse her of losing it, or take pictures from the wall and insist she had removed them. He would swing from anger to charm, confusing and frightening her so much that she began to believe she really was to blame. Because he convinced her that he still loved her and would look after her, she became more and more dependent on him, unable to see that *he* was the cause of her misery.

Well, that is pure fiction, and the Charles Boyer character was a calculating villain, yet in an unconscious way Charm Syndrome Man often behaves in a very similar fashion, controlling through manipulation.

Trevor actually did behave like the Charles Boyer character on occasions: he would deliberately hide things in order to confuse Melinda. On one occasion her son caught him doing it and told his mother. 'He had seen his father move the sugar basin from one place to another,' says Melinda. 'All the while he was laughing and smiling to himself, then he came into the living room, demanding, "Who moved this, then?" and started a big row.'

Another of Charm Syndrome Man's techniques is to imply that his partner is imagining things. One of the few places Rebecca felt she could relax and escape from Ralph's nagging over every little detail was the garden. When he was at work, she would spend hours outside, nurturing plants from cuttings. 'It was a real labour of love,' she says. 'Although Ralph didn't share my love of flowers he did help by mowing the grass regularly. But it used to sadden me that every single time he did this he would "accidentally" chop off the flower heads – usually the best ones – by just not being careful enough when he went along by the beds. To start with I used to think it was genuinely by mistake. Gradually it dawned on me that this was no mistake. Not only was it getting to be a habit, but he would laugh in my face as well if I mentioned it, and say I was mad.'

Guy could be caring, loving and tender towards Sally at times, yet emotionally abusive at others. As a result of this see-sawing behaviour, she says, 'I became very, very confused. At times I thought the abuse hadn't really happened, that I'd imagined it. There was a period of time when I didn't know who I was, I didn't know what was right, what was wrong, what was happening. I wanted to leave, but he convinced me that I was responsible for the problems, so I'd try even harder to make the relationship work.'

The Charles Boyer character in *Gaslight* was a charmer, cleverly alternating romance with anger, so that his wife never knew what to expect. It is the kind of mental torment used so successfully by torturers and terrorists who know that they can keep their prisoners compliant by frightening and disorienting them with rapidly changing moods and situations. A well-known Gestapo technique involved wearing down and confusing prisoners with torture followed by kindness. Charm Syndrome Man, on an unconscious level, does the same thing. The more the woman doubts herself and her sanity, and the more uncertain she becomes, the easier it is for her abuser to keep her under control.

Melinda described her state of mind towards the end of her marriage: 'I think the confusion was the worst thing,' she says. 'It makes one kind of paralysed. And you keep on thinking: if you try hard enough, maybe it will change.' Her account of her confusion is very typical of the way many women feel living with Charm Syndrome Man. 'I think the main effect was that I no longer knew what was real and what was not real,' she says. 'I began to lose my ability and confidence to make those kinds of assessments. I always felt that I had been a relatively strong and independent person before I met Trevor, and so I found it difficult to accept that I was in this situation, that these strange things which didn't make sense were happening to me.'

Her predicament was heightened by the response of friends and colleagues. 'They had always known me as a fairly strong-minded person who always spoke her mind, who was very indignant about violence and abuse, and I had always seen myself that way too. So they couldn't understand.

'Sometimes I would see my friends and I would be in pieces and I would want to talk about it and be comforted and get it all out, but I found it very difficult to describe what was happening because it was so incredibly violent and aggressive and frightening, and yet I was still with the man. So the attitude of my friends was: "If it's really that bad, why are you still there?" Because I didn't know the answer to that either it confused me even more, so in the end I suppose I would make light of it, because I couldn't answer the question.

'I find it much easier to understand now, but at the time I was completely confused, so I lost my base within myself. There was a period when I didn't know who I was, and I didn't know what was happening. I was so confused, and I was frightened that I had nothing of myself to fall back on, nothing that was solid and true, so I wasn't in a position to leave.

'Trevor could just switch from being lovely one moment into this kind of unpredictable, very aggressive person the next, and that was something I found confusing and frightening: not knowing when it was going to happen. When we went to bed together, I never knew whether I was going to be loved or whether I was going to be ignored, to be hit or shouted at, or frightened or put down or criticised or kicked. I just didn't know what was going to happen.

'I became very tense and anxious because he had such power, really the power that could affect me, because when somebody you love is very nice one moment and explosive and critical the next, you never know what to expect, so you can't ever quite relax. You are always frightened of a backlash. I had always been used to having a certain amount of power over what happened to me, and here I was in a situation totally without power. I had times of being incredibly angry, and wanting revenge. I was shocked by the hatred I felt towards him. Yet, two weeks after that, he could make me feel full of love and care and tenderness towards him, and that confused me a lot.

'We would have very calm times and then there were the most enormous upheavals, and it was terrifying. It was incredibly extreme, and then somehow it would go, it would dissipate. I'd be really shocked that it had happened, whereas Trevor's attitude was that either it hadn't happened, that I was imagining it, or that it was normal, and that I was the one who was unbalanced in thinking his behaviour was wrong or extreme.'

In her confusion, it was all too easy for Trevor to manipulate her into believing that she was overreacting or simply being neurotic.

Hazel likened her sense of confusion to being 'under a spell'. 'It's like they've got possession over you. You believe everything they tell you. Jimmy would say, "I only beat you because I love you. If I didn't love you I wouldn't hit you," and at the time I believed him. I used to doubt my own sanity a lot. Jimmy would say that I was frigid, that I was ugly, all kinds of things, to put me down. He knew that I never felt attractive, and he would knock me down. But then the next time he would say that I was beautiful and that I was the best mother in the world, and I was the best wife in the world. Then, in the next breath, I was the worst.'

'One of the biggest problems was the confusion of it all,' agrees Laura. 'There would be a pattern of enormous calm and togetherness and empathy and love, then there would be periods of conflict. James could be very sarcastic, very snide, very cold and very threatening. He would use his words like powerful weapons. Then he would be gentle and considerate. It was rather like walking on a volcano. Sometimes it's safe, sometimes it isn't. That confusion gave him all the control.'

One of the major weapons in Charm Syndrome Man's arsenal is this ability to be a Dr Jekyll and Mr Hyde. He confuses his partner by being abusive one minute, charming the next, blinding her to the bad times, making her forgive him, feel sorry for him, give him another chance. The most predictable thing about Charm Syndrome Man is his unpredictability. I have seen men turn up at the Refuge with flowers and chocolates. They send singing telegrams, expensive presents – anything to win back the woman and convince her that everything will change.

Hazel says, 'Jimmy would just keep saying he was sorry,

that he couldn't bear the idea of living without me. Sometimes I'd leave, and go and stay with my mother, but he'd come round and say he'd seen the light, he realised what he'd done. And I'd think, "Oh, he *has* seen it." I used to think he was really sorry, but the minute I got back he was blaming me again. I just felt that he'd conned me again, which made me feel stupid. I felt like an idiot for falling for it, but you've no idea how convincing he can be.

'And I really did want him to be like he used to be, like the Jimmy I first met. And there were lovely times. Saturdays were always special to us. I'd put on a dress and make a special dinner, and he'd do the table. We'd spoil each other. For a long time the good times outweighed the outbursts.'

Not only are they confused themselves, but most women I talk to tell me that their desperation is compounded by the fact that to friends and neighbours their abusers appear to be such good-natured chaps. To the outside world they are still charmers. Who is going to believe that behind closed doors they are making life hell for their partners? The reaction is likely to be: the woman must be crazy!

Not only does Charm Syndrome Man convince others that he is the good guy, but he cannot bear to admit to himself that he has any faults. He may not be aware of it, but it is very important to him to be seen as the perfect husband and provider.

'The most irritating, frustrating thing', says Melinda, 'was that other people always saw Trevor as Mr Nice Guy. Whenever we were in company, he was tender, he was interested, he was a really nice bloke, and very, very few people had any indication of what was going on. My own family to this day don't believe any of this, and they think that he is a really nice bloke. I mean, when I told my sister I had to call the police out, she said, "Are you sure you didn't do something?" My family would say, "Trevor loves you and he wants to take care of you, you know. Are you sure you are not making a big issue about it?" And you wonder if that's what you are doing.'

When Laura and James were splitting up, she remembers with anger that 'He used to take my particular friends out to lunch and pour his heart out and say how miserable he was. He made a wonderful victim – he's very appealing. They were quite often people he'd been very rude to before, but he managed to win them over. I thought that if I heard one more person say "Poor James" I would scream.

'They would say things like "James is really unhappy. Perhaps you should try giving him more attention," or "He really does love you, you know. Why are you so hard on him?" This was the man who was bullying me and hitting me to the point that I was a jittering wreck. When I heard the key in the door I'd start thinking, "God, he's coming back. What kind of mood is he going to be in?" And my friends were telling me I should try harder!

'He would always appear to be a passionate believer in freedom from oppression. My mouth would hang open and my eyes would widen when I heard him talking to our friends about human rights. It was sheer hypocrisy. If people had known what he was doing to me on an individual level . . . He was such a good actor. If he walked in here now, you'd probably be charmed by him. He liked to play Mr Nice Guy, Mr Wonderful, Mr Liberal . . . '

Charm Syndrome Man often distorts reality even further (albeit unconsciously) by telling his partner's friends and family that she is hysterical or paranoid. He may even threaten to have her put into a mental institution, using blackmail to get what he wants. When Laura threatened divorce, she says, 'James knew he wouldn't get custody of the children so he would say, "I will have you declared insane, you're not fit. You're just sitting around crying all the time." Well at that stage I *was* sitting around crying.'

Just as charm is the abuser's greatest weapon when it comes to winning over family and friends, and confusing his partner, it is also his trump card should the police become alerted to his violence. On one occasion when Jimmy became so violent that Hazel ran from the house and came to Chiswick, he actually went to the police and told them that she was depressed to the point of suicide, and that she had run away with the baby. He convinced them that he was afraid for her safety and that of the child.

The police went to see Hazel's sister – one of the few people who knew the truth – and she told them about his violent and unpredictable behaviour. If she had run away, she said, it would be because she was in fear for her life. The policemen's attitude was 'But he seems like a very reasonable young man.'

'I Felt So Alone'

As time went on, Melinda began to feel very alone in her relationship with Trevor. Almost without realising it, she had cut herself off from her friends, relying more and more on him for everything.

This was no accident. Charm Syndrome Man controls his partner by isolating her from family and friends and outside interests. He must be the focus of her attention. Anyone who attempts to share her love and affection is a threat. In a healthy, happy relationship, there is give and take, and both partners feel free to see friends and family, to work and pursue their own interests. But when a woman lives with an abusive man, he is the one in control, he makes all the plans and all the rules. He will encourage his partner to devote all of her time and energy to him, using his charm to make his demands seem romantic: who needs anyone else, when you have each other?

'Looking back,' says Sally, talking about the early days with Guy, 'I can see it was a sort of suffocation, but he made me feel there was no need for anyone else, we were so wrapped up in each other – that seemed to be enough. He told me I was special and beautiful and all those things, and that he didn't want to share me with anyone else.'

Charm Syndrome Man will do everything in his power to discourage friends and activities which take his partner away from the home. He may refuse to allow her to take a driving test if she cannot drive, or refuse access to the car if she can. If she wants to take a job, he will use every argument he can muster to prevent her, even if he has to accuse her of being a bad mother, deserting her children to go out to work, or put her down and ridicule her for thinking she is capable of taking a job at all.

One woman I met told me how her husband used more subtle tactics. 'I was going for an interview for a job at five o'clock,' she says. 'We were out shopping and time was getting on so I asked him to pick the kids up from school, and meet me back at Sainsbury's so we could get home and I'd have time to get ready for the interview.

'He went off, and I must have sat outside Sainsbury's waiting for over an hour – I'd got about eight bags – and eventually I had to walk about half a mile to catch a bus. I couldn't get a cab, I wasn't allowed to spend that sort of money. By the time I got home, after waiting for a bus, it was hours later, and I'd missed the interview.

'He was asleep in front of the TV and the kids hadn't even been fed when I got in. He said he'd had a look in the shop and couldn't see me, so he'd just come home. But I knew why he'd done it. I said, "It's because I was going for an interview for a job, isn't it? You're trying to drag me down." As I sat down he started slapping me and throwing things and screaming.'

What once seemed to be a demonstration of love can turn into a kind of possessiveness. 'Don't go, stay here with me – I miss you when you're away' is pretty irresistible at first, and, after all, it seems such a small thing to cancel an evening class, or a night out with a friend, but invariably these 'one-off' occasions occur again and again, until the woman begins to feel very alone. But precisely because each occasion does seem to be a 'one-off', she is often unaware of what is happening, until her isolation is extreme.

Early on in Sally's relationship with Guy she moved out of the house she was sharing with two girlfriends, and into a flat with him. One day one of her former flatmates rang to say she had an extra ticket for the ballet and asked her to come. Sally knew Guy was giving an extra tutorial that evening, so she accepted. 'When Guy rang later in the day,' says Sally, 'I told him, and there was a stony silence at the other end of the line. Then he said, "Do you mean to say you are going?" When I said that I was, he said: "I see," in a voice that sounded both hurt and accusing at the same time. He put the phone down on me and I spent the rest of the day feeling nervy and uncomfortable.

'When I was getting ready at the flat, he came back and said he'd cancelled his tutorial. He was very cold towards me and answered me in monosyllables. I finally felt I had to ring my friend and say I couldn't come. It was right at the last minute and I felt so embarrassed with my lame excuses. When I had finished the call, Guy said: "I'm glad you got your priorities right." It sounded like a warning – a sort of threat. I was bitterly angry, but I kept quiet, to keep the peace. Shortly afterwards he was all love and attentiveness; it was all right again. He made me feel it had been such a little sacrifice to make for our relationship. I dismissed it at the time – though, looking back, part of me felt that something was wrong.' Much later, Sally found out that while she was cutting herself off from the outside world and devoting all her energies to Guy, he was off having affairs with other women.

Another woman I talked to faced hostility whenever she wanted to go out with friends. On one occasion she asked her husband if she could go to a Tupperware party. Since he normally grumbled if she wanted to do anything without him, she was surprised when he said yes, of course she could go. When the evening arrived, she cooked the supper and got the children ready for bed, before getting dressed. 'I was so excited because I hadn't been out for months,' she told me. 'And I was so pleased that he hadn't said a word about it since the time I asked him. I'd had my hair done and looked out a nice dress to wear. I went up to change and put on my make-up. He came in and gave me a cuddle and my heart really lifted. I kissed the children goodbye and went out of the front door. The next thing I remember is that I was hit by water. My hair was clinging to my head and my dress was sopping. I looked up and there he was leaning out of the bedroom window with an empty bucket. He was laughing and he said, "Where do you think you're going then?" I went back into the house and cried.

'I was so hurt and angry and humiliated that I think I would have left him at that moment if it hadn't been for the children and the fact that I had no job, and nowhere to go.'

Beverley had a fairly independent lifestyle before she met Dave and had been used to having her own friends, but she admits that when they started going out together she neglected them for Dave, because she was so wrapped up in the relationship, and was flattered that he always wanted her to himself. Here we see how insidiously the normal features of a romantic relationship can blur into the beginning of controlling behaviour. Wanting to be together can lead to the man isolating the woman. This is one reason why abusive behaviour can be so hard to predict when a relationship begins. Beverley, however, after her marriage made a conscious effort to pick up again with her friends.

'Looking back on it,' she says, 'when I started breaking out and having interests, that was when Dave started getting cross.' She recalls the time she joined a badminton club with a friend, having already asked Dave if he would like to join. He had said no. 'When I came in,' she remembers, 'it was only half-past nine or something, not late, but later than he thought I should be, and he really went mad, and this was the first time I was frightened.' Beverley told me she was subjected to a complete interrogation: 'Where have you been? What have you been doing? You can't have been playing badminton all this time. Don't you realise that I worry?'

She told him that she had had to wait for a court, to which he replied, 'I don't know why you go anyway. I don't do this to you – I don't go out.' Beverley continues, 'I said,

"I wish you would. Go out with a friend." But his answer was: "I don't need to – you're enough for me and obviously I'm not enough for you." He was really very, very angry – he was beating his fists on the table, and I could see the violence within him – he was holding it back.'

Shocked and frightened at this new behaviour, Beverley rang her mother-in-law from a phone in the kitchen. This was a woman with whom she had a close relationship, yet her response was: 'Well, my darling, why do you go to these things? Why don't you stay at home with your husband? That's your place.'

Like that of so many abusive men, Dave's attitude was: If you loved me, you wouldn't need anyone else. In the end, he got his way: Beverley found it safer and easier simply to stay at home. Some abusers try to keep their wives pregnant, in order to make them more dependent on them. Frequently women tell me they are not allowed to use contraception for that very reason.

Hazel, whose husband Jimmy threatened to kill her if she ever left him and vowed, 'You'll never be free of me,' was, she says, 'always trying to get me pregnant. I mean, he thought it was really great when, a year after Mark was born, I got pregnant with twins [which she subsequently lost]. He was always forcing himself upon me when I wasn't using any contraception. It was like a sort of game or a battle, really. If I used a contraceptive cap he used to take it out and throw it across the room. And there's me frantically counting up days in my head, wondering if I was okay or not.' Jimmy's belief in his right to dominate Hazel was so strong that he even felt he had control over her body. And, ironically, although abusive men see children as a way of welding their partners to them, they are often jealous of them once they arrive.

Social abuse is an important part of the abuser's armoury. Not only will he try to keep his partner at home, but he will also discourage callers. If friends come to the house, he will create an atmosphere, so that in the end, however angry she may feel, the woman finds it less embarrassing

simply to discourage visitors altogether. 'If I had friends to
the house,' says Hazel, 'Jimmy would behave in the most
disgusting manner possible. I remember once I invited one
of the girls I worked with at the hairdresser's round for a
drink and something to eat. Jimmy refused to sit in the
same room as us for a start. He sat in the front room so
we had to sit in the kitchen, and he sat there with the
television on really loudly. And when I took his dinner
through – a perfectly nice dinner – he brought it back
in and said, "You don't expect me to eat this muck, do
you?" and threw it on the floor in front of my friend. Can
you imagine how embarrassed I was?'

Finally, Hazel says, 'I just stopped inviting people to
the house, because I didn't know how he would behave.
I began to get panicky when people called. I mean I really
did, I began to shake and I just wanted them to go. That cut
me off as well. And I didn't go and see anybody because I
wasn't allowed out anyway. I felt I had nobody.'

Rebecca told me that, as time went on, the outings to
the theatre and to favourite restaurants fell by the wayside,
and she and Ralph hardly had any visitors. She explained,
'In theory he said he liked people to come over, but he had
this way of making them feel so uncomfortable that I found
it embarrassing.' After Ralph retired, her sense of isolation
was greater than ever, because he demanded her constant
attention, and became less willing than ever to entertain
or go to see friends. She even discovered that if people
called while she was out, inviting them to dinner or to
parties, Ralph would simply decline, without consulting
her or even telling her about the invitation. Only when she
happened to bump into friends who would say 'Sorry you
couldn't make it' did she realise what had been happening.

Families pose a huge threat to Charm Syndrome Man,
because if a woman has a close bond with her parents or
her brothers and sisters, it jeopardises his complete control
over her. He will go to great lengths to discourage her from
seeing her family, embarrassing them if they call or trying
to poison his partner against them. By putting other people

down, he believes he is elevating himself in his partner's eyes.

Though an abuser rarely focuses his violence on anyone outside his immediate family circle, it is not uncommon for him to beat up his partner's mother, her sister or any relative who is close enough to be viewed as an extension of his partner. The result is that the woman feels so frightened for that person that she would rather suffer loneliness and isolation than subject a loved one to danger.

One woman told me that one night her husband started kicking her while her mother was visiting from abroad. When she heard her screams, her mother came rushing into the room. 'My husband got hold of her,' says the woman, 'and said, "*You!* You have no right to interfere – this is my house," and got hold of her arm – she was sixty–seven then – dragged her upstairs by the arm to her bedroom and locked her in it.

'Then he came back down and started hitting me again . . . the next day he told my mother she had to be out of the house. He made her change her air ticket and leave early, which was awful for my poor old mum. And from then on it was terrible, just one row after another, with him accusing me of putting my family first, loving my family more than him. The rows would go on into the night – two, three in the morning.' The result of all this was that out of fear for her mother's safety, and shame at her witnessing her husband's behaviour, the woman began to discourage visits.

When a woman lives with an abusive man, she is the one who must alter her lifestyle, and what is sauce for the goose is not necessarily sauce for the gander. Charm Syndrome Man frequently sees his own friends, and goes out on his own, leaving his partner at home, increasing her sense of isolation.

Control through isolation serves another purpose: if a woman has no contact with friends and relations, who is she going to tell when the abuse gets too much? As Melinda says, 'I had nobody.' Furthermore, Trevor had warned her,

'If you tell anybody about what I do to you, I'll kill you,' and
she had every reason to believe him. The woman is caught
in a vicious circle. Her isolation makes her more and more
dependent on her partner. She has no one outside the relationship who can give an objective view, she's cut off
from sources of support, so that if her partner beats her,
humiliates and degrades her, and then tells her she deserves
it, she begins to believe him. His are the only views she
hears. There is no one else to shed light on the situation. So
she begins to believe she is to blame, that she is somehow
causing him to be abusive.

'His Anger Cut Like a Knife'

Charm Syndrome Man can control his partner through
anger, or by withdrawing affection and attention. He
behaves like a dictator, using his anger to get his way, to
intimidate his partner. A man does not have to shout, or hit
his partner: he can show his anger by being moody or sulky.
So much so that his moods dominate the whole atmosphere
in the household. Often such mood swings are so subtle
that they go undetected by others who are present – but his
partner knows, and she feels wounded, humiliated, often
frightened. To her, his anger is as devastating as a slap in
the face.

Beverley told me that on several occasions after Dave
had been sulking for days and refusing to talk to her,
they would meet up with mutual friends for a drink, and
he would be telling jokes and chatting as though nothing
had happened – except that he would avoid any eye contact with her. 'I felt as though he was having a good time
with everyone else but me,' she says. 'I felt excluded. But
no one else would have noticed. I'd keep trying to get him
to look at me, but he wouldn't. I used to feel so tense and
edgy. So I would just stand there, not saying anything,
while everyone thought Dave was such good fun, and I
was really boring.'

Other men use anger to embarrass their partners in front of other people – so that rather than be made to look foolish, they turn down invitations and unwittingly comply with their partner's wishes by spending all their time with them.

Sally told me of a time when Guy started a row in the middle of a crowded restaurant, then walked out – leaving her scarlet with embarrassment – and with no money to pay the bill. Another time, they had had an argument on the way to a concert, which he tried to continue once the orchestra had started playing. Aware of people's irritation around her she whispered: 'Please can we talk about it later?', but his reaction was to slam his programme loudly on to his seat and storm out, while everyone was saying 'Ssshhh!'. She was left squirming, to find her own way home after the concert.

Most of us get angry at some time or another, say things we do not mean or act petulantly. But the difference between an 'ordinary' row and an abusive situation is that an abuser uses anger regularly as a controlling device. He doesn't just 'fly off the handle sometimes', his anger is part of a larger pattern of behaviour. A woman needs to ask herself whether she can live with the rows, whether they are just blow-ups which are soon forgotten – or are one factor in a whole set of incidents which make her feel unhappy, frightened or demeaned. For example, is he also jealous and dominant, does he try to isolate her from other people, does he frequently try to make her look foolish and stupid?

She should also ask herself whether her partner's anger is directed *only* at her. An abusive man is usually capable of keeping his temper with his own friends, or colleagues at work, but at home he believes that he is entitled to use anger to keep his partner in check or to get his own way. He is not some inarticulate, inadequate person who is unable to communicate with others. Charm Syndrome Man has very good coping skills. In fact, he is highly manipulative and is often capable of lying and distorting reality to suit his own needs. Contrary to what a lot of psychologists believe, this is not the behaviour of someone with 'limited coping skills'. The problem is that Charm Syndrome Man is almost *too good* at coping. What he needs to do is unlearn some of these coping skills, that is, unlearn his controlling behaviour. An abuser denies his partner the right to her own opinions. He sees her not as her own person, but as an extension of himself, so if she disagrees with his opinion or challenges him, he uses anger to punish her, to frighten her into seeing things his way, and make her change her behaviour. He believes that he has the *right* to use his anger to insist that she behaves the way he wants her to. It is a way of letting her know who is boss, of intimidating.

The result is that she uses every ounce of energy forever trying to be perfect in his eyes. If she believes a certain action of hers will anger him, she will avoid doing it – but, of course, all he will do is find another excuse for abusing her, however much he may show remorse or behave lovingly for long periods.

Sally told me that, though Guy never physically abused her, she dreaded his anger. 'However much you know he is unjustified,' she says, 'it is soul-destroying. You absorb it, you *do* begin to think, "Perhaps he is right, perhaps it is my fault." When someone is really shouting at you, and they are really, really angry, you just want to curl up and die. I found I would go out of my way to avoid upsetting him, I just couldn't bear his anger. I began to think: "I'm so bad, I've made him angry. Look what I've done." It made me feel guilty, worthless, absolutely exhausted by it all.'

For many abusive men, withholding attention and affection is as effective as shouting – sometimes more so. Often women tell me they would rather be shouted at than subjected to a silence in which they feel more frustrated, alone and helpless than ever.

One woman who came to Chiswick was also deaf, and therefore already isolated. It was hard for her to communicate with anyone, let alone on such a sensitive subject, but she managed to tell me how her husband (a general practitioner, would you believe!) would deliberately hurt her by ignoring her. 'He would sulk for days if I did something he didn't like. I would be screaming for attention. I tried to shake him for attention and he just ignored me, sitting still. "Why can't you put your arms around me, why can't you?" I was begging. "I'm so frustrated, what about affection for me? I don't feel like you love me." He just wanted sex, that's all, not love.'

Some men, if they do not get their way, will maintain a wall of silence for days, ignoring every desperate attempt at communication or reconciliation on the part of a woman. They will come around when they are ready. Meanwhile their partners feel lonely and demeaned by their rejection.

Rebecca told me of her frustration when Ralph, instead of arguing a point, would frequently just withdraw. 'It was worse than anger,' she says. 'He would cut off, and I can still see him now, walking upstairs with a cup of coffee in his hand to his own study, with the back of his neck *rigid* and a face like that, this is my vision of him. And he used to say, "'I am self-controlled when we are having a row. I am controlled and I go away."'

Almost like a father controlling a child, Rebecca felt that Ralph was putting her in the position of forever having to try harder to gain his approval. He had the power to punish or reward her every word and action, and she never knew which it would be.

'No one Understands About Fear'

One of the most powerful ways in which abusive men control their partners is through fear. Even where no physical violence is involved, their unpredictable moods can instil fear into their partners.

However, many of the women I talk to are literally afraid for their lives, or for their children's lives, or they are afraid that, whatever they do or say, they will be subjected to more pain. People who have had no contact with women who live with violence find it hard to understand how they can stay in such a situation, but, as Melinda explains, 'They don't realise how trapped you are and how frightened you are.'

She recalls the moment when her husband Trevor, the man who had 'devastated' her with his charm, hit her for the first time. 'It was when the baby was crying in the night, and I got up to look after him,' she recalls. 'I was sitting cuddling him and Trevor came downstairs and told me to put him down and let him cry. I didn't want to and he slapped me.

'I didn't even really know about violence, that men hit women. If you read about it, you don't want to know about it – you forget it, shove it away. You don't think it will happen to you. I wasn't accustomed to being frightened by men. I wasn't accustomed to being frightened of anybody or anything before this. He terrified me. I felt really scared, and I felt that I'd got myself into something which I had no control over.'

It is now two years since Melinda summoned up the courage to leave Trevor, yet she confided to me, 'I'm still very frightened of him, and I will be until he's dead.'

I have seen women whose faces have been slashed with knives and battered with hammers. One woman who was attacked with a hammer and chisel had to have 250 stitches in her face. I will never forget her as long as I live – there was not an inch of white skin, just a mass of cuts and bruising. I had to feed her through a straw.

Other women have had boiling water poured over them, or suffered miscarriages because their husbands have hit them in the stomach while they are pregnant. Hazel had six miscarriages in all after her husband beat her. One man broke his wife's arm in three places and raped her three days after her baby was born, bursting her stitches.

These women are paralysed by fear. Above all it is the unpredictable nature of the violence which is most terrifying and debilitating. Remember that the abuser changes his skin like a chameleon: one minute he is vile, the next caring, comforting and charming. Charm Syndrome Man may cry, beg forgiveness, or promise that the abuse will never happen again. He may even threaten suicide if his partner leaves him.

Laura remembers that, when James first began to be violent towards her, he appeared to be in agony over what he had done. 'He would beg me not to leave him,' she says. 'He'd say that I was the only one who could help him, the only one who understood. And if I left him, he wouldn't be able to go on. He said he'd make it better. He'd never, ever hurt me again . . . but of course he did.'

Melinda recalls, 'After that first time, when Trevor hit me, he seemed to be as shocked as I was. He kept saying: "My God, I didn't mean to do it. I don't know what happened to me." He seemed so distraught. I just wanted to make him feel better about it. Make it all right again.'

An abuser can be kind, considerate and loving for such long periods that the woman minimises the pain, even puts it out of her mind, or blames herself for causing it, vowing to be more careful in the future. But, as Laura found, after a period of calm, and without warning, some trivial incident would trigger the violence again. Gradually, the woman finds herself becoming more nervous, more wary, more afraid, never knowing how her partner is going to behave. Shot through the pattern of control is unpredictability.

Melinda told me that, as the abuse began to escalate, Trevor would go out with friends until three or four in the morning, while she lay awake 'terrified', never knowing whether or not he would decide to assault her when he came home. 'He would say, "What are you frightened about? I only beat you once a month."' Melinda recalls, 'At that time it *was* only once a month. And I'd say, "Because you could hit me *tonight*. It doesn't matter that it's only once a month, it might be tonight, and it's the waiting and the winding up that's the worst."'

For Melinda, like most women in this situation, one of the most terrifying things was that, after she had been hit once, she always lived in fear of it happening again. An abuser does not even have to strike again. Once he has instilled that fear he has all the control. 'I couldn't win,' Melinda goes on. 'If he decided he wanted to beat me up he would find anything . . . the soap would be on the right side of the taps instead of the left, that sort of thing. If I wasn't respectful enough . . . The two or three times I did stand up to him, I nearly got killed. I mean he would throttle me unconscious, so a lot of it was fear. When he told me he would kill me if I told anyone what he did to me, I had no reason to doubt him. He'd done such awful things.'

Hazel too ended up living in fear of Jimmy, unnerved above a.l by the unpredictability. Like so many abused women, she says, 'I used to hope that he would change, or that I could somehow change him – that hope went on for a long, long time. He had a belt, and he used to hit me with that, you know, the buckle, and he'd use it if I didn't get out of the room in time. And he'd keep a knife by the bed. Towards the end of the marriage, the abuse got more severe, and it got more frequent. I was demented, absolutely terrified. I just didn't know who to turn to. In fact I was thinking about suicide towards the end.'

Hazel had been to the police, to her priest, and to the social services – all of whom had failed to help her. The best offer she had had was to put her children into a home – leaving her on the streets, because she was eligible for housing only if she had her children with her. So she was left to handle her terror alone.

Once, Jimmy tried to choke her, at the same time ramming his knee into her so hard that she later had to have surgery for a ruptured spleen. 'My head was buzzing, and my ears were popping, and the *fear* . . . his face was totally distorted,' says Hazel. 'I just wanted to close his eyes, I didn't want them to be the last thing I saw when I died. I went to close his eyes, but he thought I was going to claw him, and he got up and he went in the other room. Now he had kept his air rifle there, but I had hidden the pellets, so he couldn't shoot at me – he had tried that before. But he kept a pickaxe handle up there. He'd said it was there in case there was a burglar because there had been a lot of burglaries, and he came back with the pickaxe handle and he said, "Right, you're going to die this time."

'He went to swing with it and I put my hands up and grabbed it, but I wasn't strong enough to keep it off, and it went across my neck. I had a mark across my neck for about six months. I told him I would do anything he wanted if he'd let me loose. And as soon as I promised that I would do anything he wanted, he stopped and he went to the toilet, and he was ranting and raving so much that I crawled down the stairs and got out to the front door, and he never heard.

'It sounds strange, but what I wanted to do was to run underneath a hedge, curl up and die. I was so frightened. I didn't want to die violently, but just in my head I wanted to die. I was so blind, frightened with terror, I kept running towards the fields, I just wanted to hide under the hedge, that was all I could think of.'

Eventually, Hazel ran to a friend's house. She took her to Jimmy's sister, who called the police. But even then she was too frightened to bring charges.

An abuser can instil fear into his partner simply be threatening, or hinting at it, sometimes in many subtle ways, such as driving recklessly or clasping his hands around her neck, ripping out phones so that the woman has no contact with the outside world, swearing and shouting, pounding his fists on the table, or slamming lids on to saucepans while she is cooking.

This is psychological abuse: a kind of mental torture which keeps the woman on edge, never knowing when her partner's threats and insinuations are for real.

Acts such as shouting or smashing possessions might not seem terrifying in themselves but if the woman knows that at any time, they could signal physical violence against herself or her children, that is a very different matter. She spends all her time avoiding the anger which frightens her so much. She is controlled by fear.

Melinda told me of a horrifying moment when Trevor, who was over six feet tall and weighed seventeen and a half stone, threatened her in the kitchen. 'He took a knife out of the drawer and held it against my throat.' she says. 'Then he waved it about and he said to me, "I'm going to stick this up your vagina and turn it around until there's nothing left." And I looked at his face and he was like some wild maniac. And I thought, "My God!" He didn't do it, but I believed he was capable of it.

'I think it was at that moment that I made up my mind that if he ever threatened me like that, or hit me again, I was getting out and that I was never ever going back, no matter what he said or did.'

Abusive men often play with 'weapons' in front of their partners to instil fear. Hazel's husband kept a knife by the bed. One man kept an axe under his pillow, threatening that if his wife ever tried to leave, he would use it. In the end, she was so terrified, she could not sleep at night for fear that if she so much as turned over in bed, her husband would lash out with the axe.

Laura's university-educated husband had beaten her so badly – on one occasion she miscarried after he hit her in the stomach and locked her out in the freezing cold – that even after they separated he could terrify her with phone calls threatening to harm both her and the children. One minute during these calls he would appear calm and rational, the next he would scream at her, 'Fucking bitch! I'm going to come and kill you all!'

'I mean, I had to go and get an alarm system put in,' she says, 'because I was so terrified that he would come round in the middle of the night over the roof, through the attic, or break in through the basement and come and kill us all. He threatened to do it, and I knew he was capable of it.'

Finally Laura taped some of his calls and played them back to me. What made them particularly chilling was the menace in James's voice. He would tell her, 'If you want a quiet life, do as I say, or else . . . ' So powerful were the tapes that Laura played them to her solicitor before going to court, to convince him of the kind of abuse she was being subjected to. 'He had obviously heard all this kind of thing before, and it didn't really strike home,' says Laura. 'Then I said, "Look, please, please listen to these tapes," and he did listen to them and I could tell that they had swung it completely in his mind. He said, "Right, what you need is an injunction. I can tell the sort of man he is." It just made it seem real for him, rather than hearing another story about a domestic row where a wife had got hit.'

Charm Syndrome Man unashamedly uses the threat of violence to frighten his partner into staying with him. 'If you try to leave, I'll find you and kill you' is a typical threat. Hazel says, 'Jimmy had me totally convinced that he would kill me, and that nobody could save me. All throughout my marriage I was totally convinced – afterwards when I'd got out of it, I was still totally convinced that he would come after me one day.'

Frequently women like Hazel are frightened not only for themselves, but for family, friends or their children too – because Charm Syndrome Man frequently involves them in his threats. Often the women I talk to show tremendous courage in staying in intolerable situations, rather than put their families at risk.

Jimmy knew that if he involved the children when he became violent towards Hazel, he could always remain in control. 'The time he fired at me with his air rifle,' she says, 'Mark, my son, was in the kitchen. I hadn't got him out – you know when you run in blind panic – and he was screaming, so I couldn't run away, and I couldn't run back while Jimmy was firing. So I waited until he ran out of pellets, then I ran across to get Mark, and Jimmy went and gave me a good hiding, and just kept Mark because he knew I couldn't get away because he had the bairn. Whenever he had the children, he knew he had me because I wouldn't leave the children.'

Another woman who telephoned me in desperation echoed the terror many women feel in this situation. After a particularly vicious attack, sparked off by her having cooked something her husband did not like for dinner, she could not take any more of his violence. She had gone upstairs to throw a few things into a bag, and the next thing she knew she was being thrown over her daughter's bed and flung down the stairs. Her husband told her that *she* could leave but not the children – and the catch was, if she did go the children would be dead when she got back. So obviously she stayed.

Three days after this, during which time, she says, she shook with fear, her husband agreed to leave.

'It was all sorted out. Everything was going okay,' she said. 'He'd moved out and I was happy, and then he turned up out of the blue. He was on his "I love you, I need you" routine, and asked to come back. I said no because I had no regrets over what I had done at all. He didn't get violent this time, but his temper was so bad that I could hardly move with fear.'

At the time she rang me, she and her husband were still living apart, but he constantly turned up threatening her. 'I'm frightened to go for a custody or restriction order,' she told me. 'As once he finds out, he'll smash my door down, kill me and take the kids, and they'd go through a living hell if he had them.'

However paradoxical it may appear, women in this situation often feel less frightened staying with their abusers than if they leave them. At least, they tell me, they have some idea of where they are. They feel they have some element of control over their situation. For example, in one of the most sickening cases of violence I have encountered, one woman whose face was scarred from knife attacks, came to me after being so brutally attacked that her skull had been exposed. Although she had actually run away from her live-in boyfriend, she confessed that it was almost a relief when he tracked her down. The subsequent beating she suffered was less terrifying than never knowing when he might pounce down a dark alley, or break down the door in the middle of the night.

Knowing that there is someone out there with one thing on his mind – to kill you or beat you – is one of the most frightening things any woman can go through. Women tell me that it dominates everything: they cannot think about anything else, only the idea of being tracked down and hurt again. Even when they have ceased to live with them, such men are still able to control their partners mercilessly.

Often the threat of violence is directed at other targets close to the woman, such as family pets or personal possessions. Hazel said that Jimmy 'told me he would get me and I felt he would – it was a definite threat – because he had no compulsion about killing anything. I mean he would kill an animal. I had a dog called Raffles and he shot her in the head. He'd been out with her and a younger dog, and Raffles came home before him, and when he came home he shot her in front of me and the boys. Because she defied him by coming home early.' If a man kills a pet, what is to stop him from killing his wife?

Trevor alternated between threatening Melinda and taking out his anger on her possessions. This may seem less frightening than a physical attack, but the abuser is in fact being very selective in his violence. He is in control. He will not smash anything that will affect his own enjoyment, he will never demolish his own possessions. His violence is centred on his partner and, by destroying the things she loves, he hurts and frightens her by implying that she could easily be the next target.

Melinda says, 'The place that we lived in when we first married was my flat in my name, and every stick of furniture was mine, so he used to take pleasure in destroying everything that was mine, that I'd spent so long in getting together. He used to throw my glasses across the room and break them, and punch the pictures and that sort of thing – punch the walls, put his fist through the wall – never', she notes, 'the television or anything like that.'

Another woman I talked to told a similar story. On one occasion, she revealed, after she had returned home slightly later than expected from visiting her sick mother, she found 'all my clothes taken out of the wardrobe, and ripped up on the floor – everything'. Many women tell me their partners have ripped or cut up their clothes, and they find it a particularly humiliating form of abuse. One woman told how her husband would rip her clothes with a Stanley knife, while she was actually wearing them.

It is impossible to underestimate the effects that fear, bound up as it is with intense emotions, can have on a woman – especially when the situation is confused by the fact that, however frightening these men can be, this is only one facet of their characters. They are perfectly capable of reverting to being charming, kind and sometimes full of remorse. Sometimes they do not even need to be charming: just a period of being calm and 'normal' seems like bliss to a woman who has just suffered horrifying abuse.

Melinda is well aware that, while she stayed with her husband, her fear was tied up with bewilderment, because he was able to switch to love and affection so easily. 'He confused me,' she explains. 'He got round me so success-fully with his utter contrition. I felt trapped, very trapped by everything.'

Frequently, when battered women talk to me over a period of time, there are days when I have to remind them of the horrors they have previously recounted, because in the period after the violence their husbands and partners have been kind and loving, and the bad times seem temporarily a thing of the past.

Melinda, like most of the women who come to the Refuge, knew only too well how hard it was to try to explain this to people. She had almost lost her job twice, because she was so badly beaten that she repeatedly failed to turn up for work. Though her husband had warned her, 'If you tell anybody what I do to you, I'll kill you,' when her job was threatened for the second time, she did try to explain to her bosses what was happening. But she found, 'In the end, people got fed up with me, because they didn't know how difficult it is to get away. They couldn't understand. They'd just say, "Just tell him to go. He's horrible." And they think you're not strong enough. I think they thought I was silly.

'They don't realise about fear.'

'The Bedroom Was a Battleground'

For many women sexual abuse is often the hardest of all to bear, because it violates such an intimate area of their lives. They feel defiled and humiliated, and it is often hard for them to talk about their experiences. When a woman is in bed with her partner she is often at her most vulnerable. If he violates their sense of closeness and trust, she feels attacked at the most intimate level.

Laura, like most of the women I talk to, found it desperately difficult to erase from her mind images of the sexual abuse that James had inflicted on her. At least, she told me, 'Physical abuse is sort of clean, if you know what I mean. Sexual abuse is so personal and so much the opposite of what it's meant to be, I suppose. There you are, two people together, and you're supposed to be gentle and loving to each other, and you have the exact opposite going on.'

In a loving relationship the sexual act is a shared thing, an expression of love and togetherness. In an abusive situation, the sexual act is about power. It is about a man's control over a woman. He may use it to show her who is boss, to punish her or to show his contempt for her. One woman told me, 'My husband would tell me that making love to me was like going to the toilet. He only did it to relieve himself. So can you imagine that in the back of your head? All the time he is making love he is only doing it to relieve himself!'

Sexual abuse can take many forms. It can involve physical, emotional, psychological and verbal pain, often all bound up together. A man may force a woman to take part in acts which she finds degrading and offensive, such as anal sex or group sex or even sex in front of the children.

He may threaten violence if she refuses sex – Lisa, the deaf woman, says, 'You had to do it, or you got hit' – or he may insist on sex *after* violence – like Beverley's husband, Dave. 'I could never understand it,' she says. 'There's nothing sexual about violence. It certainly doesn't turn me on, it petrifies me. And that's the last thing I'd want to do when he'd had a go at me.'

Many men actually wound their partners during sexual acts. I have even known women who have had bottles forced into their vaginas. Laura told me: 'James would hit me while we were supposedly making love, or he'd say, "I demand my rights," and hit me and I would say, "This is not the way to go about things," and he'd say, "Yes it is, and you're going to smile while you're doing it." And I think I found that the hardest to cope with, and also the most long-term thing to get over.

'The first time it happened he came into the room when I was dead asleep. My daughter was in bed with me, because I was still breastfeeding her. James dragged me out of bed by my hair across to the spare room, threw me across the bed, and shoved his penis in my mouth. And I'd been dead asleep, and suddenly to be dragged across the room like this, and thrown on the bed . . . I just bit as hard as I could.

'I thought, "Jesus, he's going to kill me now," because, you know, I'd done it instinctively, and you do such stupid things. I put the light on because I'd thought he's not going to kill me if he can see me, so I put the electric light on and I was absolutely terrified. Obviously he didn't kill me – he just roared and shouted at me and said, "Don't you ever bite me again," and I quaked and shook.

'When I think about it now, I think, "Why the hell didn't I just walk out?" I know people will think I was crazy to stay – but I had nowhere to go, no job. And there was the baby. The way he treated me made me feel so dirty and worthless as well. I suppose you could say I felt exploited. Anyway, I just couldn't think how I could begin to tell anybody. Who would understand?

'The other thing was – and I know it's hard to believe – in between the horrible bits, he'd have phases when he was so gentle and loving, that I'd put them to the back of my mind. But eventually it got to the stage where I was terrified of having sex with him, because I didn't know how it was going to be.

'Eventually, I burst into tears in front of my aunt, who made me tell her what was wrong, and it all came out. She was so horrified she said, "Right, you're leaving now," and I did – but without her financial support I doubt if I could have managed. My aunt is a wealthy woman, so she was able to find me somewhere to live, and she bought me a car, so that I could get my independence back.

'It wasn't just the money, though. Emotionally I was in such a state, I literally couldn't think what to do next. By that stage, I could barely even decide how much milk to order in the mornings, let alone what I was going to do with the rest of my life.'

Hazel's husband combined violent sexual abuse with verbal abuse, calling her filthy names, which she could not bear. 'That abused me mentally, the filthy language. And because I had been sexually abused, the filthy language seemed to fit, do you know what I mean? If it fits, you believe it.'

Often men use verbal abuse to degrade a woman when it comes to sex: telling their partners they are frigid, that they are useless in bed or suggesting that they are lesbians. One woman confided, 'There was a little girl, she was about ten, who used to come around because she used to play with my son, who was eleven. But my husband used to say, "Why is she here? Are you a lesbian?" It was just an excuse to start on me again. So in the end I couldn't have anybody to the house.'

Many women do not actually know that they are being sexually abused, because they bear no scars, and their partners have never forced them to do anything they found degrading. When I asked one woman if her husband had ever sexually abused her, she replied, 'No, not really . . . except when I was off the pill for one month between one pill and another, and because I wouldn't favour him when I was off the pill, he thought, "Well, you're my wife, and you'll do as I say," and that was it.' Like many women, she was expected to have sex with her husband, as and when he wanted it. That is a form of sexual abuse. *She* is not in control over what happens to her body – *he* is. When a woman lives with an abusive man, he controls their sex life. They have sex when he wants to, without any consideration for her feelings.

It is very easy for people to ask, 'Why doesn't she just say no?' But as Sally says, 'The times I did say no, there would be hysterics. He'd accuse me either of being frigid, not caring, or having an affair with someone else. In the end giving in was the easier option. But it made me feel as though I had no control over my body. I was just an object, to be used, as and when he liked. I'd never felt that way before. I don't think I thought of it as "sexual abuse" – I just knew that I felt bad about it. I had never thought a man could ever make me feel that way, which was even more disturbing.'

Melinda, too, was unaware that she had suffered sexual abuse, yet she told me, 'After Emma had been born – that's my youngest – I'd had a Caesarean, I'd nearly died, I'd been desperately ill and when I came home from hospital he insisted on making love to me the morning I got back. And I was in terrible pain. *Nothing* was further from my mind, and he just insisted.'

Laura told me that towards the end of her marriage James demanded sex without any regard for her feelings. 'I remember', she says, 'that he demanded sex after my second child was born. It was far too soon and far too brutal, and in a way I knew it was a test. It wasn't nice at all.' She was hurt and angered by this incident, but she had learned to bottle up her anger, she was worn out after the birth of her baby, terrified of James's reaction, and she so much wanted a peaceful, happy home for the new baby, that she gave in to James's demands.

One woman was suffering from pneumonia and toxaemia after having her first baby. Her husband did not even bother to come and visit her in hospital, yet as soon as she came home he forced her to have sex. She had had seventeen stitches, which broke. 'I was too ashamed and frightened to go back to the hospital,' she told me. 'I couldn't have stopped him, but I thought they would tell me off.'

Rape within a marriage is something we are only just beginning to talk about in this country. It is a crime for a complete stranger to rape a woman down a dark alley, but if a man forces a woman to have sex against her will in her own home, and the man is her husband, that is within the law. An Englishman's home is his castle: apparently he can do what he likes behind his own closed doors.

Unfortunately our society still endorses that view: women are still brought up to believe that they should be ready and willing to satisfy their partner's every sexual need as part of their wifely duties (and that often includes things they find distasteful). Many women accept this idea without question, because they have been taught that a man must not be allowed to feel rejected, or his ego will be wounded – he may even become impotent. And abusive men insist on their 'conjugal rights' without ever stopping to consider that their partners might like a say in the matter.

I say, what about an English*woman's* home being *her* castle? A woman should be able to say no. She should never have to give in to sex simply because she is scared to refuse, or because it is her only way of preventing a row – otherwise it is rape.

Looking back, Hazel is in no doubt about what was happening to her. 'I was being used. I mean, they say you can't be raped in marriage, but you can.' She recalls one night when Jimmy forced himself on her. Incredible as it may seem today, he insisted, 'I am your husband and you have to give it to me. You can't refuse your husband. It is my right to have sex with you.'

'He jumped on top of me,' says Hazel, 'and I said "*Uh*" and shut my eyes, thought of England – thought of anything, but I was fighting him, because I didn't want him near me. At that stage he was really punching me, holding my arms down on the bed. He was raping me. There was a knock on the door. It was so lucky. I pulled him off and said, "Look, it might be my dad," and he just went really quiet and something snapped in his head and he stopped. I jumped off that bed, threw my trousers and jumper on and I just flew out of that flat. I don't think anybody can believe how you can be abused. Eventually I just couldn't take it any more.'

Paradoxically, women often do not want to say no to sex, even though they are not really in the mood, because they hope that the sexual act might revive the loving, caring side of their partners, the side they fell in love with. The charming side. Even if they have no choice in the matter, this may be the only area which offers a brief respite from the physical and emotional abuse which colours the rest of their relationship.

Sometimes, because a couple's sexual relationship remains good, a woman blinds herself to the realities of what is happening in other areas. She is confused: how could he make love to her so passionately if he did not really care for her? That is exactly the argument Charm Syndrome Man uses. If she threatens to leave he will say, 'How can you doubt the way I feel – look how good our sex life is.' Even after the most violent rows, he will try to control his partner by making love to her tenderly and lovingly, encouraging her to forgive and forget his bad behaviour.

'Ralph seemed to think that all he had to do, after he had been really angry and abusive, was sweep me off to bed and make love to me – and it would be all okay in the morning. No further discussion required,' says Rebecca. 'That was the last thing I wanted to do. I wanted to talk things through, and make friends properly. I always felt cheated. I never had a chance to have my say – it was just assumed that all I needed was sex. That was his answer to everything.'

Just as an abusive man uses sex as and when he wants it, he can humiliate and wound his partner's feelings by *refusing* to make love to her. In a healthy relationship one partner might be too tired to make love, or simply not in the mood, yet there are ways of saying no, without hurting the other's feelings. An abuser, on the other hand, will tell his partner she is frigid, ugly and undesirable, that she does not satisfy him or that he should never have married her. If *he* has sexual problems, he will blame them on her. Or he may put her down, calling her a slut for making the first move, leaving her feeling guilty, confused and rejected.

Often an abusive man backs up this rejection of his partner in bed by ogling other women in front of her, and making unfavourable comparisons when they are out together. She feels humiliated, and her self-confidence fades, so that even when he is loving and gentle again, she finds it very hard to respond.

While such battles are going on in the bedroom, abusive men are frequently also being unfaithful – though such behaviour would be unthinkable in their partners. One man sexually abused his wife a few weeks before he left her for another woman. 'I thought he was going to make love to me in the normal way,' she says, 'and I partly reacted, but then he started being violent and then he threw me on the bed and attacked me from behind and he penetrated me from behind – it was terrible. He was a big man and his weight on me hurt my left hip, and it was many months before the strain was relieved, I had to have treatment from an osteopath for it. So that was absolutely disgusting. He said because he was in love with this woman, he couldn't have sex with me in the normal way, because it would be adultery, and only with this woman he loved was it normal.'

This man was very calculatedly humiliating and de-grading his wife, in order to remind her who was in control. The more ashamed and demeaned she felt, the more superior he felt, and the more he was able to dominate her.

Many men continue to behave in this way, even after they have separated from their partners. Women frequently tell me that their husbands and boyfriends come back, under the pretence of collecting belongings or seeing the children, and then rape them – as if they still have to prove that they have the upper hand.

'He Controlled the Purse Strings'

An abusive man will try to control the purse strings, just as he tries to control every area of his partner's life. Traditionally, it is the man who is seen as the provider, the head of the family, who goes out to work to feed his wife and children. Many women are perfectly happy with this, since their husbands and partners are generous and open about financial matters, and they do not feel frightened to ask for their share.

An abusive man, however, uses the giving or withholding of money as a symbol of his power over his partner. If their income is low, and she is unable to work because they have children, he will constantly remind her that she cannot survive without him. Not only does that idea reinforce his control over her, but it often prevents her from leaving.

Even women from comfortable backgrounds can be trapped in the same way. It is a myth to assume that such women have their own resources, or easy access to joint funds. Many women who live with abusive men have to ask their partners every time they want to make a purchase, often having to submit minute details so that a decision can be made about whether or not they are *allowed* to have a new coat or a pair of shoes.

Even if a woman has an independent career, it is not unusual for an abusive man to manipulate her into a situation where he is in control of their finances. Or he is so extravagant that she has to bail him out of financial trouble. She is often dependent on his 'generosity' for every penny she has for herself, the children or the housekeeping, and even in less extreme situations, if a woman looks carefully at her life, she usually realises that *he* makes the decisions about how and when to spend money, even if she is the breadwinner. Not only is he controlling the financial aspect of their relationship, he is also tying her to him more irrevocably. If she is dependent on him for money, it is so much harder for her to leave.

Sally happily used her student grant to buy king prawns and fillet steak to satisfy Guy's love of good food; she even delved into her grant to buy petrol for his car. Yet, she recalls, 'On one occasion he got hysterical because I asked him for twenty-three pence to buy some tampons. By this time my grant money had almost run out. I didn't think it was unreasonable to ask for a box of tampons out of his money. At the time I was really furious, but he was so busy ranting and raving I didn't get a word in edgeways. Eventually I let the whole thing blow over.

'Another time when I had finished studying and was working, we were on holiday with friends in Scotland and I bought my niece a woolly hat for one pound fifty, which was a real bargain. He rowed about this for three days in front of our friends, even over the dinner table. He maintained *we* couldn't afford it (even though I had my own income and bank account!) and put me down for being frivolous. Privately my friends said they couldn't believe his reaction.'

Many abused women tell me that their husbands and boyfriends spend all their money on things for themselves, leaving their partners struggling to buy things for themselves and their children. One woman told me, 'My husband was getting a cooked meal at work every day, but he wasn't giving me enough money to buy food at home. Some weeks I just had my family allowance and the lady at the corner used to take milk tokens in exchange for food, so I'd be buying potatoes and bread and things like that with my milk tokens, and with my seven-pound family allowance getting nappies and that sort of thing. And just eating lots of chips and bread.'

Like Sally, this woman was also humiliated when she asked for money to buy tampons. 'He wanted to know how much they were, and when I came back he held his hand out for the penny change! He said: "It's *my* change – I want it."'

Jimmy's money went on drinking and smoking and playing the fruit machines, yet Hazel felt guilty about complaining, because he frequently turned the tables on her, reverting to the man who 'could charm the birds out of the trees', spending extravagantly on her, buying her a new jacket, a handbag or perfume.

Charm Syndrome Man is frequently careless with money – he will insist on romantic weekends away, or expensive meals, even though he and his partner are broke. Then he will blame her for the fact that they have no money, and expect her to bail him out of trouble.

One woman, in her sixties, who had been subjected to emotional and sometimes violent abuse for years, told me her husband was 'very childish with money. In the end I was the manager and ran the bank accounts.' She was the main earner, but that did not stop him from feeling he had every right to spend all her money. 'When I first met him,' she says, 'he had nothing. He didn't even have a car, so I had put more into the marriage financially than he had. I also earned more than he did. When he was out of work for two years, it didn't even occur to me to think that I was keeping him; it was just one of those things.

'When I was fifty-five I was offered early retirement – you get a lump sum and one-third of your salary as a pension – I'd thought about it and I didn't really want to give up work, but I remember him looking at the pension details and saying, "*We* will get this lump sum, *we* will never get the chance to get our hands on a lump sum like that again. We'll invest it." The more he talked about it, the more I thought, "Well, why not?" So I took early retirement the following September. The day after I put the money in our joint account, he bought a new car, a Rover 2000.'

Shortly afterwards, this woman's husband abandoned her for another woman, sexually assaulting her before he went. 'When he left home he took what remained in the account,' she says. 'He said, "It was out of the joint account, therefore it was mine." I was left with nothing. He also took the car, leaving me with his battered wreck, which I've still got.'

She had had no idea that her husband was seeing another woman, and despite the fact that he often slapped her and regularly put her down, she loved him, trusted him and was totally committed to their future together. The last thing that had entered her head when she was making her financial arrangements was that he might empty their bank account and leave her. His behaviour left her both financially and emotionally shattered. Later, to twist the knife even further, he deliberately became unemployed, so that he could not be made to support his wife. Even when he abandoned her, he was still exercising control.

'I Must Be to Blame'

Charm Syndrome Man puts his own interpretation on events, twisting the emphasis so that his partner is to blame for his own abusive behaviour.

'Jimmy blamed me for everything – it was always my fault,' says Hazel. 'He said I provoked him. If I hadn't argued with him, nagged him or upset him or whatever you want to call it, then I wouldn't have been hit. He always twisted it around afterwards so that I ended up comforting *him*, to make him feel better for what he'd done.'

Hazel suspected Jimmy was having affairs. 'But', she says, 'if I asked him about it, he told me I had a wicked mind. After a while you think you *must* have a wicked mind, you know. Everything was my fault. I mean it was my fault because I answered back, it was my fault he couldn't find his cigarettes, it was my fault he didn't get his cigar – if the shops were closed it was my fault. I mean I used to go around apologising.'

The abused women I talk to almost always feel guilty and ashamed. They feel that they have failed in their relationships, that they must have in some way caused their partner's abusive behaviour: 'If I hadn't done this, If only I had kept quiet, if only, if only . . . ' One woman whose husband had abused her for fifteen years – he frequently held knives to her throat and threatened her with his gun – said to me, a whole ten years after she had escaped to a remote Scottish island, 'Actually I think I was partly to blame.'

Hazel was tortured by such feelings: 'I was frightened for a long time that it was something in me that attracted this in him. I thought I brought it out in him. Even after I left him, I would be feeling guilty. Now I've realised that it wasn't me at all – because friends have told me he behaves even more badly with his second wife.'

When Melinda first contacted me, one of the first questions she asked was: 'What part do I play in the abuse?' Trevor had convinced her that she was to blame for his behaviour. ' I think what kept me very confused', she says, 'was the guilt. I thought it was all my fault. That is what Trevor used to tell me. He'd say he never had arguments with anyone else.

'There was a whole period of time in which he had told me that it was my fault, that it was my behaviour that caused his violence towards me. If I had had a couple of glasses of wine with dinner and he was abusive later, he would say I was drunk and had provoked him. He said our friends didn't like coming around any more because I was irritable – I'm sure I was on occasions, but is it any wonder when I was living on tenterhooks all the time, not knowing how he would behave?

'And because I was cut off from myself, I was cut off from

the outside world, I was cut off from all my friends – anybody who knew what was going on in that relationship – I suppose the only logic seemed to be to believe it *was* all my fault.' If only she could change, or stop provoking him, she believed, the abuse would stop too. As she says: 'If Trevor was telling me it was *my* fault, and making me believe that, then, if it was *my* fault, I could also make it better.'

Because women like Melinda are so isolated, they are frequently unsure of themselves. There is no one to tell them that they are not to blame. All sources of support are barred to them. 'The crazy thing', says Melinda, 'is that Trevor was the one who would comfort me after the abuse. He would tell me how lucky I was to have someone as caring and understanding as him to look after me, which only made me feel guilty for having wanted to leave.

'I used to search and search and search for what I had done wrong that caused the dreadful abuse. It must be my fault, it must be something I had done, how could I change it? That idea that it was my fault became the cornerstone of the relationship – and it was only when I was able to talk to people who made me see that I wasn't to blame that I began to build my self-esteem and confidence and get out of the very tight web of that relationship.'

Hazel took her guilt one stage further: 'I blamed myself for marrying him,' she says. 'I felt it was my own fault. I blamed myself all the time. I carried the burden of this guilt and shame around with me. But now I realise I didn't deserve to be treated like that and nobody does. No human being deserves to be treated like that. But there are a lot of women still trapped by guilt.'

Many abusers involve the children, to make their partners feel even more guilty. One woman told me that her daughter came to her and said, 'Couldn't you try to be nicer to Daddy?' 'He had completely poisoned the children against me,' the woman told me. 'He told them that the rows were all my fault. That he didn't know what to do. He'd tried, but I was impossible . . . Can you imagine how I felt? Frustrated, hurt, angry and guilty.'

It is not unusual for an abuser to tell the children, without foundation, that their mother drinks too much, or does not look after him properly – leaving the woman feeling she is to blame not just for the abuse, but for tension in the house. If he behaves badly in front of the children, she frequently feels guilty for not protecting them from such scenes.

Not only do abused women feel guilty within their relationships, but it is often guilt which prevents them from leaving. They believe that it is wrong to abandon their partners and split up their families, however bad their situation is. They feel guilty at putting themselves first. Invariably they have been brought up to believe that a woman should put her man and her relationship first; she should make sacrifices, and take the rough with the smooth.

Ralph frequently reminded Rebecca of her 'duty'. 'He would tell me that if I left I would have failed, that there was something wrong with me if I couldn't cope with a little bit of his anger, and that it was all part of the ups and downs of a relationship, it was part of the rough and tumble of family life, and that I should see it in that context.' Had this been a 'normal' family life, with 'normal' ups and downs, Ralph might have had a point – no marriage runs smoothly all the time – but when a woman lives with an abuser, the downs are not in the least 'normal'. They are destructive and demoralising.

However, because Rebecca wanted the marriage to work, she says, 'I tried to have that attitude as well. I could still look at him and see what a nice person he was, what a caring, loving, tender person he was, and what a good father he was to my children and I wanted to make all that work. I felt it should be my responsibility,' she says. Bewitched by the charm, she felt she was to blame for the abuse. Ralph's control was complete.

3

The Abused Woman

What Stops Women from Leaving?

'Why does she stay with him?' is invariably the first question everyone asks when they hear that a woman is being abused by her partner. They think it should be so easy to walk out, slam the door and never return. But for most abused women it is not that simple.

Anyway, many women *do* leave (a British survey showed that 88 per cent of abused women left home after assault), but somehow we always find ourselves concentrating on the women who are unable to leave.

'Why does she stay?' is a question which always irritates me because I find it irrelevant. After all, if a woman's partner turns out to be a spy or an armed robber, would people immediately ask, 'Why does she stay with him?' In such a situation, people immediately recognise that such a man's behaviour cannot be tolerated, and should be prevented. So why should the focus be different when the issue is woman abuse?

Because the woman is the target of that abuse, you might say. But my whole thesis is that a woman does not cause her partner to be abusive any more than she might cause him to be a spy or a robber. And his behaviour – even if it does not involve physical abuse – is no less intolerable.

Why a woman stays with an abusive man is not the point. The real issue is: Why do men abuse women in the first place, and how can we prevent it from happening?

Whenever I hear someone say, 'Why does she stay?' I tell them they should turn the question around and ask, 'What stops her from leaving?' 'Why does she stay?' implies that there is something wrong with an abused woman, that she is somehow different from other women, that she is somehow responsible for ending the abuse. That of course is a myth: just as perfectly innocent airline passengers can become hostages in a hijack, a woman can unwittingly find herself in a relationship with an abusive man. And once she is caught up in the Charm Syndrome, it can be very hard indeed to get out. 'Why does she stay?' also suggests that a woman has control over her life – but it is Charm Syndrome Man, like a hijacker, who has all the real control.

It is important to understand the enormous odds a woman is up against, in order to see that the real point is not why she stays, but what a triumph it is when she is able to leave. Indeed, it is a miracle that she can cope with her predicament at all, at the same time as looking after her children, holding down a job, maintaining her sanity and so on.

Never forget the power of the Charm Syndrome. One of the major effects of Charm Syndrome Man's behaviour is an overpowering sense of emotional dependency between him and his partner. He convinces her that the two of them are bound together in a kind of symbiotic relationship, in which each depends on the other for their very existence. This dependency is so powerful that most women don't want their relationships to end. It is only the bad times which they want stopped.

After a period of abuse, most women quite naturally are looking for affection, reassurance and calm. Because they are usually so isolated, they feel that there is often no one who can offer a shoulder – except their abusers themselves. As Melinda told me, whenever she needed comfort after the abuse, there was Trevor putting his arms around her, telling her he would look after her. When their partners reveal the comforting, tender and loving side of their characters in this way it is hardly surprising that the women are drawn back towards them.

Charm Syndrome Man does not see his woman as an individual, but as an extension of himself, and frequently she comes to believe that too – for better or for worse. She believes that *he* needs *her*, that without her he won't be able to cope. Some abusive men are so bad at organising money that their partners believe they cannot manage financially without them. Many men threaten to commit suicide if their partners leave them, and the women believe they are capable of carrying out their threats.

Since women are brought up to be the caring sex, when a man is violent and then pleads and cries and promises to change, a woman almost invariably reaches out to help and comfort, rather than turn away. Beverley told me that Dave had her trapped emotionally for a long time. 'He told me, or made me feel, that he might commit suicide, that he didn't know what would happen, he didn't know how he would cope, and obviously because I cared for him I didn't want to do him that damage,' she says.

'The whole situation is so complicated and complex. I should have left Dave years ago, for his sake too. As it was, I mothered him for twelve years and he became more and more helpless, so at forty he ended up with no job and no money, nothing. But it's very difficult to leave somebody who you know loves you very much and is dependent on you, no matter how bad it is at times. Whenever he pleaded with me to forgive him, it really got to me. I could see how much he was hurting, and I wanted to make it all right.'

At other times, it is pure fear which prevents a woman from leaving her partner – fear that he will come after her or her children if she tries to get away. Often it is a mixture of fear and love. One woman, who had one small child and was pregnant again, told me she was scared to tell anyone about the times her husband battered her, because she believed that they would take the children away. Many women are also terrified by the thought of having to go to the police or to take legal action against their partners.

Another fear is that of being alone. Many people are worried about being alone, but when a woman is being abused by her partner, this fear is often heightened because abusive men dominate and control their partners so much that they have convinced them that they are unable to cope on their own. These men have been at the centre of all their emotions – good and bad – for so long, how will they fill that vacuum? However badly treated they may be, fear of loneliness can often outweigh fear of abuse, particularly in situations where the battering is either infrequent or emotional and verbal rather than physical.

Melinda explains, 'I think it was fear that made me stay for so long, fear of a whole lot of things. Fear of him finding me if I left, fear of failure, failing to make the relationship work. And during the last year I felt frightened of being on my own, which I had never been before. I was really bothered about it. How would I cope with the children, the practicalities of it? I felt frightened of losing the continuity, the kind of intimacy you have when you are living with someone.'

Ironically, even though she lived with a man who could viciously beat her at any time, Melinda was still more frightened of being without his protection against strangers. 'I would feel frightened that somebody was going to break in, that somebody was going to attack me, because I was on my own,' she says with a wry smile.

Even where there is no physical abuse involved, an abuser controls and dominates his partner so effectively that he can often convince her she is to blame for the abuse. So she is trapped by feelings of guilt and shame. She feels she must have done something to deserve her ill treatment, so instead of leaving she tries to change. Or lives in hope of her partner's charming side reappearing permanently.

Often it is easier to stay than to accept defeat and face the outside world. 'There's still such a stigma about divorce,' says Rebecca, especially among the circles we moved in. Single women always seemed to be an embarrassment. Nobody knew quite what to do with them. There was always so much emphasis on couples that I felt that they would think I had failed if I left.'

If the woman has children, the issue is complicated still further because she may have been brought up to believe in the two-parent ideal at all costs. And Charm Syndrome Man exploits this to the full. Rebecca says, 'Ralph said to me that if we split up my children would be deprived of a father again. He convinced me that it would have a detrimental effect on them.'

An abused woman may be frightened of independence, of being without a man. Women constantly say to me, 'How will I survive without him?', 'Will I ever find anybody else?', 'I'm forty and not used to being single.' They say these things because they have been brought up to think in this way. They may even stay to preserve their husband's reputation, to avoid ruining his career.

Abused women are frequently isolated from friends and family. They have no one to turn to and nowhere to go. They may have little or no contact with an outside world which could show them their predicament from a different viewpoint. Even career women who have contact with people every day still feel so humiliated and ashamed by the fact that the person they are closest to is treating them abusively that they keep their problems to themselves. The result is that they are more dependent than ever on their abusers.

They do not stay with their partners because they are some kind of masochists, or because they just give up and give in. They are often very angry, but their partners have prevented them from expressing their anger for so long that they are unable to use it constructively.

Melinda, like many women in her position, see-sawed between wanting to reach out to Trevor to comfort and be comforted, and feeling so angry and frustrated that she fantasised about revenge. 'I would plot these kinds of fantasy ways I could make him suffer, or ways I could eradicate him or blot him out by killing him,' she says. 'I would lie awake at night and watch him sleeping and I would imagine shooting him or plunging a knife into him, and I was quite obsessed by the feeling,' she admits. 'Or I would fantasise that he'd been in an accident on the motorway and killed or disabled, because if it happened like that I would not get found out, whereas if I attacked him in some way, I'd be guilty.'

Many women feel this way. They feel they have so little control over their situation, that the only way out is to actually kill their partners or themselves, or somehow to will their abusers to go off with another woman or walk under a bus. Odd as it may sound, when women are in this state of desperation and confusion, of suppressed anger and fear, leaving does not seem final enough. They feel that just walking out of the door will not end the nightmare. Their partners will still come after them and threaten them, or persuade them to come home. As Melinda says, 'I felt as if Trevor had some kind of spell over me. That the only way I would ever be free of him was if he was dead.'

But no matter how often abused women dream of revenge, they rarely inflict any physical violence on their partners, however angry and bitter they may feel. Instead they tend to internalise the anger, often becoming so stressed and worn out that it is all they can do to cope from day to day, without also having to consider the enormous strain of actually trying to leave their partners. Such women have been so controlled and dominated that they have grown used to suppressing their feelings, and they often lack the self-confidence to make any decisions at all. They are frequently debilitated by a catalogue of illnesses and complaints, especially the kind of psychosomatic ailments associated with stress, such as backache, headache and fatigue.

'Over a period of time,' says Beverley, 'it was as if my body knew things were not right, things were not as they should be, and it was giving me very strong messages. For a period of about one or two years, on long weekends, or if we spent three or four days together, I would have low back pain and I would be constipated and this became a really well-established pattern.'

Since society is slow to recognise the problem of the abuse of women, studies on the effects of physical and emotional abuse are few and far between. However, there is some documented evidence of the kinds of health problems women in abusive situations experience. One report, 'Emotional and Physical Health Problems of Battered Women', concluded that women whose husbands abused them physically 'had significantly more somatic complaints, a higher level of anxiety, and reported more symptoms of depression'. And a 1975 survey of battered wives found that 71 per cent were taking anti-depressants or tranquillisers, 46 per cent of the women had consulted a psychiatrist and 42 per cent had made a suicide attempt or gesture. Two years later, a study of sixty battered women found that they almost always experienced agitation and anxiety bordering on panic. Many were unable to relax or sleep and, when they did sleep, they frequently had nightmares. When a woman is this tense, worn out or depressed, is it any wonder that she frequently does not have the strength to put together a plan of escape?

Many women are dependent on their abusers not only emotionally, but financially as well, since the men insist on handling – or, as is often the case, mishandling – the financial aspect of a relationship. The woman may be tied to the home with young children, or her partner may have refused to allow her to take a job and earn an independent wage. The result is that the woman often has no funds of her own to enable her to leave. Many women tell me their husbands have threatened to sell the house if they leave, so they will not even have a roof over their heads.

Rebecca says, 'Ralph dug his heels in and insisted he would never leave *his* home, so what could I do? I couldn't physically throw him out. When I threatened to get a solicitor, Ralph just laughed in my face. After all, he is one himself – and he knew all the tricks. He would have had an answer for everything. As always!'

When I talk to abused women at the Refuge I am constantly aware of their appalling plight when it comes to housing. Under our present system, it is the abused woman and her children and not the abusive man who are made homeless. In theory, the Housing (Homeless Persons) Act of 1985 should provide accommodation for such women, but in practice they are literally dumped in the oldest, most run-down, dangerous, dark, isolated housing estates in Europe.

In London, particularly, most of the properties offered to them have already been refused by families on council waiting lists because they are in such dreadful condition. But if a woman turns such a property down she gets no other offers. Her only alternative is to seek help from a refuge – if she even knows that they exist – but the refuges are forced to turn away thousands of women daily because there simply is not the bed space.

One woman I met had been driving around in a van for months, with her little daughter, because there was literally nowhere for her to go. Another woman, whose husband was a dentist, was forced to leave him and take her four children to the local housing department, after he had been so violent that she feared for all their lives. She was told there was absolutely nothing available: not bed and breakfast, not even a bed space in a homeless families' hostel. The result was that her four children were taken from her and put into a children's home, while she was left to fend for herself. She was so desperate that the only thing she could think of was to take the train to Gatwick, where there were cafés open and where she could curl up and sleep unnoticed.

Other women are unaware of the state benefits they can claim, or they are reluctant to put themselves in a position of being dependent on social security.

Women from other countries who are married to British men have special problems. One Latin American woman, whose husband beat her up after only a couple of months of marriage, came to the Refuge for help. Even though she was pregnant, because of her foreign status she was incorrectly told she was not entitled to state benefits or housing. To cap it all, she was advised that if after a year she was no longer living with her husband, the Home Office would have her deported. Her only options were either to become dependent yet again, this time on the Refuge, or return to him and not only face more abuse, but be labelled a masochist for 'going back for more'.

Women who have stayed at home for years with young children worry about who will care for them if they have to go out to work. They may not have friends or family who can help, childcare facilities are woefully scarce, and private nurseries very expensive.

One black, abused woman who desperately wanted to do a further education course at college to enable her to get a good job, found herself blocked at every turn. Because she was staying at the Refuge she had changed boroughs. The old borough accepted her for the course, but the fees were astronomical because she was no longer a local resident. She begged and borrowed the money to pay the fees (her sole income was about £42 per week) and arranged for a friend to look after her child. Unfortunately those plans fell through. She applied to the local authority in the new borough for childcare, and was told there were no facilities, and even if there had been, she would not have been eligible because she was not a permanent resident. Private childcare cost £55 a week, £13 more than she was earning. In the end she was forced to give up her course. The only saving grace was that we were able to find her housing, though she still has to live on state benefits, much against her principles.

Many women find themselves in similar situations in which they are shunted from a refuge into housing in a completely new area, where they have no friends or family. Their children frequently feel unsettled, because invariably they have to change schools. Often they are put into temporary, unmodernised accommodation at first, and then moved on, causing even more disruption in their lives. Sometimes the children become so desperate for home comforts, their own friends and their toys that the women give in and go home to their partners, rather than upset the children any more.

Many abused women find that well-paid jobs – particularly part-time ones – are still not that easy to come by, especially if a woman has not worked for years. On top of the fact that her skills will probably be outdated, she must overcome her nerves about making her way in a work situation after a long break.

Women from ethnic communities often face special problems. Black women tell me that they frequently feel doubly abused: by their partners and by a society which can still be prejudiced, particularly when it comes to employment. A black woman with young children to support who attempts to leave her abuser must at times feel she has insurmountable obstacles to tackle.

In many cultures separation and divorce are considered completely unacceptable. In the Asian community, in particular, it is simply not permitted for a wife to leave her husband. An ethnic minority woman may experience language difficulties and be particularly isolated. Often she has no one to whom she can turn for support. She may be ostracised by her community for contacting the police or leaving her husband. And in Catholic countries women are either unable to get a divorce or divorce is simply not recognised.

For all women, whatever their religion, or colour of their skin, the idea of having to face a marriage counsellor, a doctor, a lawyer or a clergyman is so offputting that they would often rather cope than leave. Calling the police and actually prosecuting the man for whom they have such ambivalent feelings is a huge barrier in itself – particularly when most women, many from previous experience, believe that the reaction from the police will simply be to say, 'Oh, it's just a domestic', and walk away.

Sometimes I wonder how the abused women who come to Chiswick have managed to leave at all, given the emotional, financial, psychological and social obstacles they have to overcome.

Even when they are determined to leave, if they cannot afford solicitors' fees, they find it extremely hard to get legal aid, because there are very strict rules about eligibility. Women have to prove that they are on a low income, which involves time and a lot of red tape at a period of their lives when such obstacles are especially demoralising. Even when legal aid is approved, law firms frequently do not want to take on such cases because they pay so badly. During all these delays, the women's partners frequently sell their houses and dispose of their assets.

Ending a relationship is a painful and complex process for anyone. There will be ambivalent feelings, attempted reconciliations, hopes that things will improve, feelings of guilt at leaving, anxieties at facing a new life. But for an abused woman the trauma is doubled. It is easy to say glibly, 'Women have a choice – why don't they leave if it's so bad?' But do they really have a choice? Abused women are trapped. They are women who are frightened, confused, isolated. Yet they are survivors, resilient, courageous women who in the face of a living hell cope admirably. In fact it is often because they are so preoccupied with coping and surviving in the short term that they are unable to distance themselves long enough to make the long-term decision to leave.

Survivors, Not Victims

'You can't win, so you soon learn that it's easier just to shut up than find yourself being hit or abused again,' says Hazel. An abused woman is in a situation remarkably similar to that described by hostages: her life may be in the balance; she is isolated from outside help; and the person who is in control of her life can switch to being charming, kind and comforting.

This is a very similar scenario to the one in which four employees of a Stockholm bank found themselves in August 1973, after robbers burst in and held them as hostages. Unexpectedly, these hostages feared the police more than their captors. They even developed a kind of bond with the robbers. Sociologists studying this incident called it the Stockholm Syndrome: when the hostages survived, they felt that they were indebted to their captors for giving them back their lives. According to these sociologists there is a parallel between the relationship of hostage and captor, and the kind of dependency which often occurs between a battered woman and her abuser.

Certainly, like the hostages, abused women often find themselves in ambivalent situations, not knowing whether to hate their partners or to try to reach out to them, but instinctively justifying and defending them in preference to trusting outsiders. I would say that both the Stockholm hostages and abused women behave this way because they are acting out of natural instincts for self-preservation. Consciously or subconsciously, they are aiming to survive.

It is easy to be sceptical when you are not trapped in such a position – but think about it. When a woman has been relentlessly criticised, made to feel worthless and cut off from her friends and outside support, is it any wonder that she is unable to challenge her abuser, any more than a hostage is likely to defy a captor who has a gun pointed at his or her head?

By appearing submissive and going along with their captor's wishes, abused women – like the hostages – realise, often instinctively, that they can buy themselves time while they think of a long-term strategy or an escape plan.

'Compliance' can be a way of surviving, a way of getting through their ordeal physically and emotionally intact.

Many sociologists disagree. They believe that abused women are in a state of 'learned helplessness', a syndrome described by Leonore Walker in *The Battered Woman*. Leonore Walker suggests that battered women believe that they cannot control their situation, so they become passive, submissive and helpless. The theory is based on experiments performed on various animals, particularly those carried out by experimental psychologist Martin Seligman on dogs.

The dogs were put into cages and given electric shocks at random intervals. At first the dogs reacted, but when they realised that nothing they did prevented the shocks they became passive and gave up trying. Even when the cage doors were opened, the dogs still did not respond. Finally, they had to be repeatedly dragged to their escape routes before they began to react for themselves again. The longer the dogs had been exposed to the shocks, the longer it took them to recover from the effects of this 'learned helplessness'. According to those who subscribe to the theory, abused women behave in much the same way.

In my experience, however, though women may be temporarily paralysed by abuse, often finding it difficult to make decisions or solve problems, very few give up trying to change their situation. Unlike Seligman's dogs, they do not easily accept defeat. To the outside world, because they do not immediately dash for the door, they may seem submissive and passive, but in fact, in all sorts of often subtle ways, they fight back, they adopt survival techniques and actively find ways of coping.

Imagine for a moment a scene from one of those old-fashioned cinema melodramas. The heroine is on a train, being driven by her handsome husband, who, she has discovered too late, is a murderer. She knows that in a hundred miles' time the train is going to smash into the buffers and both of them will die, but a hundred miles seems a long way off, and she knows she must survive until then. The immediate way of achieving this seems to be to find a good hiding place, so that he can't find her and attack her, while she thinks of what to do next. People along the railway line are shouting: 'Why doesn't she jump off?' 'She must like the danger,' they reckon, 'otherwise she'd escape.' And by now the woman is so frightened that she too wishes she had jumped off at the beginning, but the train seems to be hurtling along faster than ever, and it is far too difficult . . . or is it? Maybe it isn't too late to jump after all . . .

Just as she is considering jumping, her husband finds her. But instead of attacking her, as she expects, he says: 'Stay with me. I need you. If you stay, I'll steer the train to HAPPY EVER AFTER.' The woman is by now terrified and confused, but she is still able to grasp at straws. HAPPY EVER AFTER is where she always wanted to live, after all. The relief of not having to jump off the dangerously speeding train, and the fact that her husband now seems remorseful, gentle, and kind, and is offering her warmth and love makes this seem the better option.

But, just as she is beginning to relax she realises that the change of direction was only a loopline, and that she is back on the main line to CHAOS, with her husband laughing and threatening her once more, and the train travelling faster than ever . . . She realises she has no choice: she has to jump and risk the consequences. When she recovers from her leap, she is confused and bruised, but she is safe and FREE.

A pretty dramatic analogy, certainly, yet when a woman lives with an abuser she behaves in a similar fashion. All her energies are devoted to immediate, short-term survival. It is difficult for her to see the picture as a whole: the idea of leaving her partner is as nerve-racking and dangerous as jumping from that train. Yet, like the woman on the train, rather than being a pathetic, passive victim, she is a resourceful and coping survivor.

The abused woman is in a situation over which she has no control, yet she cannot accept that; she believes she can change things, that by altering her own behaviour, she can bring out the loving side of her partner, the side she fell in love with. So she adopts every strategy she can think up. It is only when she finally realises that she cannot alter her abuser's behaviour, that – however charming and gentle he is capable of being at times – he will always revert to abusive behaviour, only then can she summon up the strength and courage to jump off the train.

It is a mistake to assume that abused women do not fight back or stand up for themselves. The women I talk to adopt all kinds of strategies to survive. Sometimes they are subconscious, almost reflex actions, sometimes they are deliberate plans for survival.

The most universal instinctive way that women cope at one time or another during their relationship is to do what their husbands and boyfriends do: they minimise the problem, deny it altogether or actually forget that it happened – because it is simply too painful or problematical to deal with. This is known as denial and I will go into it in more detail in the next chapter.

Hazel, like many abused women, had her own special survival tactics. She had hair long enough to sit on, but after her husband grabbed it and pulled her around the house by it on several occasions she had it cut short to prevent him from doing it again. Another ploy was always to sit on the chair nearest the door – 'ready to run'.

Laura hid the kitchen knives, while Beverley kept a set of clothes in a bag near the stairs and another in the battered car she refused to sell – just in case. 'I was holding on to my sanity,' she says, 'I was holding on to my possessions, which I thought were my life.'

One woman told me that when her husband started a row the first thing he would do was reach for the wooden hangers in the wardrobe and hit her with one – so she replaced them all with plastic ones. Another woman was repeatedly raped by her husband, who came home every night drunk. One night she hid a carving knife under her pillow and, after he had raped her, she held it to his throat and said, 'If you ever do that again, I'll kill you.' After that, she moved into the spare room and they never slept together again. This woman came off lightly – most abusers take revenge if their partners challenge them in this way.

Abused women often cope by adopting their partner's political and social views, to steer clear of confrontation, or they adapt their behaviour, avoiding scenarios which have led to verbal or physical assaults in he past. Like the hostages in the Stockholm bank, they appear to outsiders to be colluding with their abusers, yet they are acting almost instinctively out of a sense of self-preservation.

Hazel says, 'I used to keep my face timid and say nothing, so he couldn't put me in the wrong and have an excuse for hitting me. You learn over the years not to challenge them, so they don't kick you about. Sometimes I'd curl up in a ball, hide in a corner, just to try and stay out of his way. I was forever saying to my family, Don't say that because he'll get annoyed and don't do this because he won't like it . . . '

One woman adopted a whole set of survival tactics, ranging from carrying a key to her neighbour's house in her pocket at all times, to deliberately keeping quiet, never speaking unless her husband spoke first, so that he could not accuse her of starting an argument. 'I got clever, I had been with him so long,' she says. 'When he started shouting and hitting me, I'd stay as long as I could to make sure the kids were all right, and to see if he'd calm down. If he didn't I'd put my coat on and say I had to go out for cigarettes. I had arranged a secret meeting place with the kids – at a café nearby – so whenever I had to leave, they knew where to find me. I also made an arrangement with my next-door neighbour that if ever she heard screams, she would call the police.'

Many women learn to lie, to be deceitful, to avoid their partner's displeasure. Jimmy would be furious if Hazel wasted food. 'He got cross if something went bad in the fridge and I hadn't used it,' she says. 'He'd shout, "It's a waste, it's a waste!", so if I did find something, I'd wrap it up in tin-foil and hide it in the bottom of the bin with something over the top of it. You become very secretive – not because you're a secretive person, but to avoid their wrath.'

If Rebecca was busy with the children, and unable to have the supper ready by the time Ralph came home, she would put a stockpot on to the stove so that the smell would fool him into thinking his meal was cooking. 'Otherwise,' she said, 'there would be a row.'

The point about survival techniques is that they are never long-term solutions. They help the woman cope with her immediate predicament while she gathers the strength and makes plans for the final separation. But they can never solve the problem, because *nothing* a woman does can alter an abuser's behaviour. Only *he* can do that.

Sally, Melinda, Rebecca, Hazel, Beverley and Laura, like all abused women, had to make up their minds to leave in their own time. First they had to recognise that coping and surviving is only a short-term measure – that, by being brave, abused women simply become part of the denial conspiracy.

4

The Denial Conspiracy

Whose Problem Is It Anyway?

One of the most striking aspects of the problem of woman abuse is that there seems to be a great conspiracy on the part of the men and women involved, and on the part of society as a whole, to pretend that woman abuse is not really a problem at all.

'He denied everything'

Abusive men frequently deny their abuse outright, suggesting that the women are making it up or that they are crazy. To the police, neighbours, family, they will say, 'Of course it isn't true. She's imagining it.' And, because they can be so charming, they sound only too plausible. Hazel says, 'Jimmy denied everything. If Jimmy said something didn't happen, it didn't happen. I mean, he denied ever hitting me, and as far as he's concerned, he hasn't.'

Guy, like many abusers, simply lied whenever Sally suspected he was having an affair (which he was), making her feel guilty for even suggesting such a thing. 'One day,' she remembers, 'a woman phoned up and seemed confused when I answered the phone. It seemed she was the mother of one of his mistresses – she claimed that Guy was actually engaged to her daughter! I can still hear her now saying, "That man is like a ram rushing up and down the countryside!"

'When Guy came home I confronted him with what she had said, but he told me this girl was some crazy student who had a crush on him. He told me that in his position these things happened all the time, and I shouldn't give it a second thought. It was me he loved, etcetera, etcetera. And, probably because I wanted to, I believed it. Do you know, I found out later that he had actually been a member of a dating club!'

Melinda says, 'Trevor would absolutely dispute that he was ever physically violent – even though he had knocked me down, kicked and slapped me. He said it was just my fears and fantasies. I even had a friend who had been physically abused by her husband – much worse than me. She had had broken arms and broken legs, and Trevor was very sympathetic towards her. I tried to say that she wasn't very different to me – even though I had no broken bones, the way he made me feel was the same: the fear, the intimidation and the frustration. But he couldn't see it.'

Even if Charm Syndrome Man does not actually deny his actions outright or insist that his partner is crazy, he will deny responsibility by minimising the seriousness of his behaviour, and suggesting that his partner is over-reacting or exaggerating. 'I barely touched her – she just bruises easily.' 'It was only a little slap,' or 'I didn't hit her *that* hard' are well-used lines.

Even if an abuser admits to his behaviour he will make excuses. 'It wasn't my fault – I was drunk' or 'You know I didn't mean it – I'd just had a bad day at work and I took it out on her' are typical. Charm Syndrome Man will blame alcohol, a sudden loss of temper, jealousy, the fact that he is unemployed, miserable at work or worried about money – anything and everyone but himself. And, more often than not, first in line for the blame is the woman he has abused.

Even if a man accepts what he has done, he will often attempt to *justify* it. 'I was provoked,' he will say, or 'She brings out the worst in me.'

'I told myself it wasn't really that bad'

It is not only the man who denies and minimises his behaviour – the woman frequently does the same thing, partly from fear of recrimination from her partner – remember how Trevor threatened to kill Melinda if she ever told anyone – and partly because they are afraid of facing up to the problem because, once they do so, they will have to face up to difficult and painful feelings.

They will have to admit that the person they love – or once loved – most, the charmer who seemed so wonderful, is somebody entirely different: callous, unreliable, controlling. And once they recognise that, they feel they must do something about it. How can they accept all this and not act? They are caught in a double bind: to leave or to stay, when neither option seems to be the answer. Rather than face such decisions, it seems easier to justify, excuse and minimise their partner's behaviour. The irony is that by doing so they allow their abusers to get away with it.

Many women (as I suggested in the previous chapter) use denial as a positive way of surviving from day to day, while they gather strength to leave. It is a tactic often adopted by people in difficult and distasteful jobs. They push away painful feelings. If they crack up, they feel, they will be no use to anyone, so they temporarily shut out the greater implications and dangers of their situation and concentrate on the particular job in hand.

One psychologist calls this 'psychic numbing' and likens it to the behaviour of the survivors of Hiroshima, who, though they were perfectly aware of the devastation all around them, found a way of coping by closing themselves off and numbing themselves to the horror.

When Guy denied that he had been unfaithful to Sally, she says, 'Subconsciously, I trained myself to believe it. You've got to survive and avoid aggravation. And if he had admitted that he had had affairs, I felt I would have fallen apart. I couldn't stay with someone who was unfaithful. I would have had to do something about it, and I suppose I wasn't ready to face up to that.

'I even managed to let him convince me of the most bizarre things! On one occasion I came home from work to find a used condom in the waste-paper bin in the bedroom. He came in at that moment and when he realised I had seen it he actually said he'd been masturbating and didn't want to stain the sheets! When I look back, it's incredible that I preferred to let myself go along with it, rather than cause another row. It is amazing the way he managed to put his own slant on everything.'

When women first come to me for therapy, it can take a long time before they are actually able to remember many of the things that have disturbed them most. For many women 'forgetting' these things is a way of coping, while they gather the strength to deal with their predicament. Even after they have been talking to me for a period of time, there is still this inclination to 'forget' the bad times. There would be occasions when I would have to remind Melinda that Trevor had beaten and abused her, because in the interim periods he had been so caring and attentive that, consciously or unconsciously, she had blocked out the bad memories.

'It frightens me now,' she agrees, 'but during the good times I lost my ability to remember the abuse. I would try and think about the times when he had hit and kicked me, and in a way I would find myself believing Trevor's perception of it. It was as if I had imagined it, that it didn't really happen or that it couldn't have been that bad.

'Even the extreme situations like the time after my mum's funeral when he threatened to push me under the train, and the time when I had a miscarriage and he shouted at me and told me he was going to leave me, and he was aggressive and abusive for three weeks afterwards. Those kinds of things I just couldn't remember, until after the relationship ended, and then they all kept flooding back. I would be doing something and suddenly I'd remember and think, "Oh God, what about the time he did that . . . "

'I had always thought that I could speak up for myself

against any wrongs or injustices that were being done to me, but in this kind of crazy situation I didn't. Because I felt so incredibly reduced as a person, and because I found it so hard to accept that I was in this situation, I suppose I went along with Trevor's view of things, because it was a way of coping. If I was going to stay with him, then I *had* to believe it. I was so completely confused about who I was and what my feelings were that it seemed easier in a way to cope with the outside world by isolating myself and not expressing what was happening.'

Often women keep quiet about abuse, because their partner's controlling behaviour has ensured that they feel too guilty and ashamed to admit what is happening. Rebecca says, 'I didn't tell anyone for a long time, because I was embarrassed. I didn't want anyone to know that this so-called perfect relationship was really nothing of the kind.'

'The shame was very, very strong,' says Laura. 'I was terribly middle-class. To my friends I developed this strategy of not talking about things. I just told them the same old story about everything being fine. I was reluctant to tell anyone because I wanted people to see us as a pair and a family. I didn't want to admit what was really happening. Also, I had the whole thing about feeling guilt – you know, thinking I must have brought it on myself somehow.'

Melinda says, 'I was so ashamed of it that I didn't tell anybody until the last time when Trevor marked my face so badly that I couldn't hide it. You tend to block out the bad things. You can't actually remember the details. And I think I had the idea that no marriage is totally wonderful all the time. That's what I told myself.'

Most relationships, of course, *aren't* wonderful all the time – but there is a difference between a healthy relationship which has its ups and downs and one where a man consistently abuses his partner, where he makes her afraid to be herself and unable to do the things she wants to do, and where she has to deny and minimise whole chunks of her life.

Blaming herself is another way of minimising and denying

in order to cope. If a woman feels she is to blame for her partner's behaviour, it follows that by altering her behaviour she can stop the abuse. In believing this, a woman can believe that she still has some element of control over her situation. For many women, the idea of accepting that they are completely powerless to change their partner's behaviour is just too frightening to accept.

'He must have had a good reason'

So the abusers and the abused deny – but society also denies and minimises the problem of woman abuse by going along with Charm Syndrome Man's excuses. It is easier for society to believe that a man abuses a woman because he has had too much to drink or is jealous than to take a long hard look at itself and see if, perhaps, there is more to it than that. If it did see that, it would have to do something about it. Often, too, like the survivors of Hiroshima, society finds it easier to pretend that the abuse is not happening, to 'numb' itself to the reality, because it is simply too appalling to face.

Society also denies the problem in its reluctance to become involved in what happens between a man and a woman behind closed doors. People feel awkward and embarrassed, and do not want to interfere. 'A man's home is his castle,' we say, as usual, and regard interference as an invasion of privacy.

Friends and families are often reluctant to intervene in cases of physical abuse – even though these same people would probably rush to dial 999 if they saw a stranger being attacked on the street. And as long as the community turns a blind eye in this way, a man's castle will often be a woman's prison. I find this attitude extraordinary. After all, if a burglar was to say, 'Sorry, I only rob people when I've had a bad day at work or I'm on drugs,' who would listen?

There are some people, of course, who think women are not really that important anyway. In the recent debate over whether or not to abolish mandatory life sentences for murder, a *Times* editorial (25 September 1989) noted that 'murderers vary from remorseful men who, when quarrelling with their wives, have gripped or hit too hard – to robbers going armed with intent to shoot their way to their spoils if necessary.' In other words, there are murders and there are murders, and when a man murders his partner it is a 'crime of passion' which is somehow excusable.

There is a statistic which I think speaks volumes for the recognition society gives to the problem of woman abuse, and that is that there are some 1500 registered shelters for animals in this country (and many more unregistered ones), but only 200 refuges for women. Such refuges as do exist are overcrowded, understaffed and underfunded, and most of them are in big cities – not much help to women living in country areas. Nor are there enough helpline services for abused women.

There are more examples of the way in which society turns its back on the problem, and in doing so perpetuates it by denying women an escape route. The response of the police, social workers and relief agencies is often woefully inadequate. The approach is too often that the woman is to blame, and the onus is on her to prove otherwise.

We see this attitude frequently in the case of rape. It is a measure of how little attention society pays to the rights of women that a woman frequently has to convince a court that she was not to blame for the attack. It will be suggested that she provoked it by walking alone late at night or wearing short skirts. Some judges even give more lenient sentences where they believe this to be the case. Other judges have given light sentences where they have decided that the woman's trauma was not that great. What we fail to recognise is that rape, like assault by men on their partners, is a calculated act of violence and has nothing to do with uncontrollable sexual urges. At some point the rapist makes a choice and, whatever one feels about the woman's behaviour, she cannot force him to rape her.

The police are the main agency who can deliver a

clear message: to abusive men that assaulting a woman is a criminal offence for which they must pay; to abused women that they do not have to put up with abusive behaviour; and to society that such behaviour is criminal and should not be tolerated.

Yet, in the course of my work, I never cease to be amazed at the number of men who go scot-free when they have inflicted the most brutal injuries on the women they live with. In Canada, my home country, there is a vigorous arrest-and-prosecution system, yet in Britain I continually encounter the most unsympathetic treatment of women by the police. Invariably, they blame the woman or back away from becoming involved in domestic incidents. In doing so, they are reflecting society's denial.

In 1986 the Police Monitoring and Research Group reported that responding to domestic violence was 'at the bottom of the police list of priorities' and that due to a 'cult of masculinity' in the force, 'a policeman is more likely to identify with the wife-beating man than the besieged woman' (*Cosmopolitan*, January 1988).

One woman told me how she escaped from her husband, who had attacked her with a chisel. She ran into the street, with her child in her arms, with blood streaming down her face. As she did so she spotted a police car, and with relief flagged it down. When she told the two male officers that it was her husband who had inflicted her injuries, they told her there was nothing they could do, and drove off. Her case was never investigated.

Another woman, a widow in her sixties, met a man she wanted to marry. Then one night he attacked her, ripping a hank of hair from her head and knocking her out by slamming her head against a table. On her emergence from hospital, she asked the police to take action. When they heard it was her fiancé who had attacked her, they refused. It was only after seven months of lobbying and complaining that she finally secured an arrest. Hazel told me that, on one of the numerous occasions when she called the police, she was frightened and hysterical, which prompted one of the officers to tell her, 'Calm down, or we'll put you away.'

Another woman told me that while she was separated from her violent husband he turned up hammering at the door and threatening her. She was terrified – she tried to phone her father, but discovered that her husband had got in earlier and cut the wires inside the mouthpiece. 'I thought, "I'm trapped. I can't get out of the balcony. I can't jump one floor. I can't phone anybody to tell them," ' she told me. 'So I kept the children in the living room and kept them quiet and I was looking out of the kitchen window, which is away from the street-door landing, and I happened to see a neighbour. I only knew him to say hello to, but I shouted down, "Excuse me, please ring the police – my husband's a bit violent. Please, please ring the police."

'I felt so low to have to swallow my pride and let somebody know what was happening to me. I thought, He'll go upstairs and think, "Stupid person, she's a bit mad, shouting out of the window that her husband's attacking her" – but he did call the police. My husband was shouting, "You slag, you whore, who have you got in there?" and I heard the police coming so I opened the door. They took him away, but I discovered later that they didn't take him to the police station, they dropped him off around the corner at his local pub. He told me later, "Oh, the police were great. They said, 'Look, just play along with us, jump in the car. Where's your local?'" And they dropped him off outside.'

Another time, he pounced out of the blue, while she was returning from the shops pushing her baby in her pram, with her son walking alongside. 'I thought I was safe in the street,' she said. 'I thought, "He wouldn't start in the street." Then: slap, punch around the face with the back of his hand. He grabbed the pram, and I wouldn't let go, and I said no, and I was crying. With that he hit me so hard I let go of the pram, and he ran off with the baby. I thought, "What do I do? My baby – he's got my baby – he's violent – is he going to hit her?" So I phoned the police.

He'd taken her to his brother's. I ran round there and the police turned up.

'Apparently I just screamed, I was in such a state – I wanted my daughter back, and they just said, "There's nothing you can do. She's in safe hands, she's with your husband, and the house is clean and everything. Promise us that you'll leave it alone and you won't come back." I said yes, but I was in such a state, I wanted my daughter back, so I went back, and begged him through the door. All of a sudden the police turned up and said, "Look, if you don't go back, you're going to be arrested." I said, "What for? I'm doing nothing wrong in wanting my daughter back," and they arrested me.

'The most humiliating thing was going into the police station, having to take my wedding ring off, my clips out of my hair, as if I was going to do something drastic. They wouldn't allow me to smoke, and I had to turn out my shopping bags. One was really nasty as if I was a criminal – I felt like I'd mugged an old lady. They said, "We won't keep you – you're going to go to court in the morning," and I thought, "I've never been to court in my life. Why are they doing this to me?" I was petrified, because I didn't know what it would involve. The judge was awful . . . I was bound over to keep the peace for two years in the sum of £25.

'The police arrested *me*,' said the woman incredulously, 'yet they drop *him* off round the corner at the pub.'

I come across this dismissive attitude all the time. On one occasion when a particularly violent man kept turning up at the Refuge, I telephoned the police station, because there was a warrant out for his arrest. The duty officer was extremely patronising. He told me, "Don't worry – I know him. He wouldn't *really* hurt her. He knows when enough's enough." So for that particular policeman there was an acceptable level of physical abuse.

There have been some signs of change. The Metropolitan Police have issued an order to their officers drawing their attention to their powers of arrest in domestic situations, and there are now thirty-one specialist units dealing with cases of woman abuse. Current figures show that the arrest rate for assaults in the home has risen by 165 per cent since the order was issued in 1987 – but the reality is that only a tiny percentage of batterers who are arrested are actually charged with assault. And, even when they are charged, the number of abuse cases which actually end up in court, compared with other cases of violent crime in the community, is negligible.

Even if the police are sympathetic, the Crown Prosecution Service frequently decides that there is not enough evidence to continue, and the case is turned down. Invariably, too, the judiciary refuses adequate injunctions to women and accepts undertakings from the men that they will curb the violence. And, as we know, Charm Syndrome Man is very capable of winning people over to his side with his professions of remorse and promises to change.

In theory there are a number of court orders designed to protect abused women, but in practice these are constantly broken. Recently one husband followed his wife to the Refuge at midnight, and was banging on the door, threatening to kill her. She was so terrified that the doctors gave her tranquillisers. She had obtained an injunction, with powers of arrest, so that in such a situation the police could step in immediately. They did so, but instead of being held overnight and taken to court the next morning to be dealt with (which was the purpose of the injunction) he was released after five hours. He came straight back to the Refuge and resumed his threats.

This man's threatening behaviour alone was a criminal offence – even without the added weight of the injunction – yet *still* he was allowed to go away scot-free. The examples I could include on this subject would go on for pages and pages.

Instead of pushing for prosecutions to help cut back the cases of women abuse, the authorities stack the odds against a woman. In one case, the Crown Prosecutor turned to an abused woman, who was armed with perfectly adequate evidence against her partner, and suggested, "This case is going to be very stressful for you. Do you think you ought to change your mind?" Having gone through so much actually to arrive at this stage of proceedings, the woman was so worried by his comments that she was persuaded to drop the case. The Crown Prosecutor may have been genuinely concerned for her feelings – but the result was her abuser walked away, free, and the court had simply carried on where the husband had left off, undermining her courage and confidence.

In most cases it is hard enough for the woman to go ahead with a prosecution as it is – her partner may be threatening her, and agencies may be putting pressure on her to keep the family unit intact – without her feeling that she has no real support in court either.

Recently the case of Michelle Renshaw hit the headlines when Judge Pickles ordered her to spend seven days in prison because she was so terrified of her boyfriend that she refused to give evidence in court. While the sentence was held by many to be overly harsh, the judge took this action because he was determined that this man should not escape justice. His decision highlighted a system which failed to support Michelle: she should have been properly protected, counselled and encouraged to give her evidence.

The police complain that, when they do make arrests, women often withdraw charges, but it is this lack of support that is often to blame for her faltering at the final hurdle, at a time when a woman is usually being intimidated by her partner and is trying to cope with a whole set of emotions, such as fear of the future, guilt and shame – a time when she is most in need of encouragement.

Many of the conclusions reached in court appal me. One woman recently ran away from her violent husband, bringing her two children with her to Chiswick. In court the judge told her that refuges were unsuitable places for children and that if she wanted to keep them she would have to return to the matrimonial home. What could she do? She was more worried about losing her children than about the danger to her own safety, so she went back. Every day at the Refuge, we expect a phone call telling us she has been seriously assaulted – or worse.

Agencies other than the police, though meaning well, often fail abused women, too. Blaming the woman is such an easy trap to fall into that even counsellors sometimes make the mistake of asking, 'What did you do to make him hit you?' All this does is heighten the woman's self-doubt, guilt and shame, and imply that the man is in some way entitled to be violent. Her partner will almost certainly have brainwashed her into believing that she is at least partly responsible for his behaviour – now here is her counsellor reinforcing that view. Often counsellors insist on seeing both the man and the woman together, inevitably making it difficult for the woman to speak freely, and implying that the man is not entirely to blame.

'Are you depriving him of sex?' 'What did you do to upset him?' 'Did you start it?' are all loaded questions which women seeking help encounter all the time, from the kindliest people. One woman told me that the response from her call to a helpline was 'Perhaps you should pay more attention to him?' Other women tell me that counsellors have suggested, 'Perhaps you could make yourself a little more attractive?'

One physically battered woman whose husband was persuaded to have therapy told me, 'The therapist said I should treat him as a toddler, as if he had just found his feet, and just found his anger, and he was experiencing it for the first time, and that he had to express that, but gradually things would calm down and we would have a much more fulfilling, expressive relationship.' As this woman wryly pointed out, 'What she wasn't aware of is how terrifying it is to live with a man who is six feet tall, weighs twelve stone and is an expert in karate, who "behaves like a toddler" and flies off into inexplicable rages at any time.'

All these responses shift the blame on to the woman,

and suggest that the remedy lies with *her* rather than the abuser. If he is not held to account for his behaviour, then we give him permission to continue.

Some women tell me how they have been rushed to casualty units with wounds inflicted by their partners – only for their abusers to be allowed into the units with them, where they frequently tell the medical staff their own versions of the story and are invariably believed. Other women have gone to their general practitioners in desperation, only to be given tranquillisers by doctors too busy to ask enough questions. Others have turned to clergymen, only to be reminded about the sanctity of marriage and asked, 'Perhaps you are not being attentive and caring enough as a wife?'

Even the language we use implies that the woman must take her share of the blame. Instead of talking about 'woman abuse' we say 'domestic violence', 'conjugal violence' and 'abusive relationships'. Even if the woman is not blamed exclusively, the usual attitude is that she must share the guilt. 'It takes two' is such a hackneyed phrase that people never even stop to think whether it might have any foundation in truth.

Society is locked into the idea that, if a woman is abused, she is somehow responsible. Blaming the woman is almost instinctive. 'She probably deserved it,' people say, with no real knowledge of the facts, 'and anyway he only slapped her.' Or 'She shouldn't have gone on and on at him,' or 'If she were my wife, I'd have done the same thing.' Even people who are genuinely concerned to help the woman fall into the trap of diverting the blame in her direction. 'You chose him, you'll have to make the best of it,' 'He seems such a nice chap, it can't be all his fault,' 'Perhaps you both need help' – all these phrases are regularly trotted out to women by people who mean well, yet unwittingly put the onus on the woman.

Well-meaning people often practise amateur marriage counselling, but invariably they try to repair the relationship, rather than make the man own up to his behaviour.

Very rarely does anyone tell the woman – or the man – the most important thing they both need to know: that *she* is not responsible for her abuser's behaviour. No woman can *make* a man abuse her. It is a choice *he* makes. The upshot of all this woman-blaming is inevitably that *she* believes it too (after all, women are part of the same society), making it even easier for an abuser to excuse himself.

The blaming, the passing of the buck, the denial, the excuses and the justifications go on and on, round and round in a vicious circle, while women continue to suffer, men fail to take responsibility for their behaviour and our society turns a sceptical face towards the women it should be helping, preferring to believe the popular myths about woman abuse, rather than look for deeper truths which may be harder to tackle.

Instead of looking boldly in the mirror, we allow ourselves to be distracted by myths.

Myths

'He was just drunk,' 'He was jealous,' 'He's having a hard time at work,' 'He comes from a violent home' – these are the kinds of excuses I hear repeatedly when people talk about cases of men abusing women. Even more incredibly, people have asked me, 'Is it true that pollution is a cause of wife abuse?' One man even said to me, 'I hear wife abuse is on the increase because of the disastrous England football results.'

Some factors such as drink and jealousy may contribute to the abuse of women, but I do not believe that any actually *cause* it. And, what is more worrying, the tendency to write off abusive behaviour as just the result of one drink too many, unemployment or a jealous rage can actually perpetuate such abuse, because while society accepts these excuses no one feels obliged to look for the real root cause and do something about it.

I believe the reasons why men abuse women are much more complex, but before we discuss them it is important to cut through some of the myths which obscure the real causes.

'Some women are turned on by violence'

There is a whole school of thought which maintains that women secretly enjoy being abused – in fact they are attracted to it. Some people go one step further in putting forward a theory which, I feel, has perpetuated the idea that women are to blame. They believe that some women are 'chemically addicted' to violence. That some imbalance in their chemical make-up draws them towards pain.

For a start there is no medical evidence whatsoever to support this theory of chemical addiction. And the theory does not explain why men batter women. Even if this theory were correct, there would still have to be men out there prepared to abuse such women and satisfy their 'craving'. Such women could not *cause* men to be violent, only the men could make that choice. To suggest that a woman could turn a gentle, considerate man into someone who controls, subjugates and humiliates her is quite ludicrous.

Furthermore, in my experience, women usually have no way of knowing that they are embarking on a life with an abusive man. Remember the stories of our six women? When they met their partners, they each thought they had found a soulmate who was charming, gentle, kind and considerate. They had not yet discovered the abusive side to these men's characters. How could they be attracted, or addicted to violence they were not even aware of?

I am not denying that there are masochistic women – any more than that there are masochistic men – but this has no bearing on woman abuse. If abused women were really masochistic, if they were really attracted to the abuse, would they come to the Refuge for help? It simply does not make sense.

The assumption that abused women must be masochistic or chemically addicted to violence has largely arisen because many women find it difficult to leave their abusers. If they stay, the argument goes, they must like it. However, many do leave. And if they stay, as the women I have interviewed explained so graphically in the previous chapters, it is because they are trapped, and because they have been brought up to feel worthless without a man – not because they are masochists or chemically addicted.

'What about abused men?'

One of the easiest ways of avoiding an issue is to turn it on its head. So when many people are asked to face the problem of woman abuse, they insist that it is a one-sided question, that men are as abused as women. For some reason, people seem to think that if they can show that men are abused too, then woman abuse is not a problem they have to think about. It seems that woman abuse is the one crime where people instinctively leap to the defence of the offender.

As far as physical abuse is concerned, the statistics clearly show that battering is a male prerogative: 76.1 per cent of domestic violence involves husbands beating their wives, and of the remainder only 1.1 per cent consists of women beating their husbands. In America FBI statistics demonstrate that every eighteen seconds a woman is battered by her partner. As I mentioned in the Introduction, 18 per cent of murders in England and Wales are of women by their male partners. And only 2 per cent of murder cases concern women killing their husbands. Researchers Evan Stark et al revealed that approximately one in four visits by women to casualty departments were made by battered women and Dobash and Dobash in *Violence Against Wives* reported that 80 per cent of the women in their study had sought medical help for their injuries on at least one occasion. In America the statistics are even more horrifying. According to the FBI, again, one in three women murder victims were killed by their husbands or partners in 1984.

Generally speaking, men are stronger than women, and can inflict much worse injuries – particularly when a woman is pregnant, and there are then two casualties. In *Battered Wives*, Del Martin reported that 25 per cent of battered women are battered during pregnancy.

'Nagging wives are just as bad'

As far as emotional abuse is concerned, everyone must be familiar with that favourite caricature of the nagging wife, shrieking at her poor downtrodden husband – the butt of music-hall jokes, literature and popular songs.

Why is it always women who seem to be tagged with negative labels? Why doesn't anyone say: what about nagging men? After all, abusive men constantly nag, harass and criticise their partners. And abused women, contrary to the stereotype, do everything they can to avoid 'nagging' – because they are afraid of provoking more abuse.

I will not deny for a moment that a woman who does nothing but nag and criticise is unattractive and irritating, but however bitingly sarcastic, however cruel and venomous a woman may be, I do not believe that a man feels that he is being *controlled* by such a woman in the way that a woman is controlled by her abuser.

Nor is he trapped in the same way. Men who are unhappy in their relationships may stay with their partners for the sake of the children, or because their lives are predictable, if unexciting. But they do not stay because they are trapped by insurmountable social and emotional barriers. They rarely have to face the problem of trying to find good, well-paid jobs after years of rearing children. When it comes to leaving, women have far fewer options than men.

The bottom line is that men do not feel controlled

and trapped by their partners in the way that women in abusive situations do.

'She provoked it – she deserved whatever she got'

It simply is not true that the abuse most women suffer is in any way provoked by them. As we have seen many women are attacked when they are asleep. Laura was sexually abused while she was asleep. Hazel was sitting quietly smoking a cigarette when Jimmy snatched the cigarette from her hand and pulled out a lock of her hair. One epileptic woman was dragged out of her wheelchair by her husband, who walked through the door and said, 'What are you sitting there like that for?' She had done nothing, said nothing. He simply attacked her. There may be no row – nothing that a woman can put her finger on, which causes the abuse.

If a woman is particularly unpleasant, do we say a burglar is entitled to rob her home? However appallingly a woman may behave, this does not excuse abuse. A man still has a choice. He does not have to use violence, he does not have to be verbally or emotionally abusive. Frustrated as he may be, he can learn to control his anger, to walk away, to try to resolve the problem with his partner calmly, to accept that she has a right to her own point of view.

'It only happens in low-income families'

That could not be further from the truth. Abusers and abused women come from all income brackets, classes and creeds – as I mentioned in the Introduction. Remember Joel Steinberg and Hedda Nussbaum, Charlotte and John Fedders and the famous names you have read about in the press and heard about on the television.

I constantly receive phone calls from women who are married to wealthy and influential abusers, and many come to me for advice. It may be that they do not always figure in the statistics, because they do not necessarily move into refuges or contact the police for help.

'It's because he grew up in a violent home'

Many people believe that boys who grow up in violent homes will repeat the pattern as adults. There is conflicting evidence on this subject. Personally I would say that while it is true that many boys who experience abuse grow up to be abusers, some turn their backs on all forms of abuse in revulsion against their childhood experiences. Growing up in an abusive home may be a factor, but it cannot be the sole cause – otherwise all men who grew up in these circumstances would go on to abuse women.

Yes, boys in such homes do receive messages that they should be aggressive, powerful, in control, but the family is only a microcosm of society. These messages are everywhere: in children's books, on TV adverts, in magazines. Boys are given the impression very early on in life that women do not deserve respect.

The family may be a great influence – but that family is only behaving in the way that some families have behaved for generations, because our society has grown up with the idea that men are supposed to keep 'their' women in line – even to the point of being violent and abusive.

'There's a pattern of abuse in her family'

The argument is that there are women who, though they may not be chemically addicted to violence, choose violent men – sometimes again and again – because they have grown up in abusive homes and have not developed any self-esteem. If their mothers are passive, they behave the same way. Also, the argument goes, such women have only known abusive behaviour. So, subconsciously, they feel comfortable with it. It is 'normal' and familiar to them. Men who treat them well seem unexciting and tedious.

But statistics show that there is simply no correlation between a woman's background and the chances of her becoming an abused woman. Many women who grow up in loving families find themselves involved with abusive partners as adults. Hazel told me that when she met Jimmy she was hoping to find the kind of happiness her parents had enjoyed. Moreover, in my experience the last thing women do is seek out abusive men. And, as we know, Charm Syndrome Man never reveals himself in his true colours at the beginning of the relationship. So how could the women know they had 'found' an abuser?

Nor does this theory explain why men abuse women. Even if there were women running around, desperately looking for abusive men, they could not turn men who have no abusive tendencies into abusers, just to suit them.

It *is* possible that some women from abusive backgrounds end up with abusive men, but given that one in four women will be physically abused at some point in their lives (quite apart from the millions who are emotionally abused) it is hardly surprising. Nor is it surprising that some women leave their abusers only to end up with someone else who treats them just as badly. Almost every woman could find herself involved with an abusive man – whatever her background or emotional make-up.

Quite apart from the statistical odds, when a woman leaves an abuser, she frequently feels worthless, guilty and ashamed. Her self-confidence is at a low ebb, and she is often even more susceptible to the messages she receives all around her: that she must have a man to look after her, protect her and take control of things for her. In this state, it is all too easy for Charm Syndrome Man II to step in. After all, he and his partner are still part of a patriarchal society, a society which nourishes woman abuse. Instead of asking 'Why does she choose another violent man?', we should be asking 'Why does he find another woman to batter?'

'He must be sick'

Very often, people's instinctive reaction when they hear of a man abusing his partner is: he must be crazy, or he must be socially or sexually inadequate (one abused woman, married to a journalist, said to me, 'Surely there must be an organic base to his problem?'). These are understandable reactions, since to accept that the man is not sick, that he is just Mr Average, is an idea that most people – particularly women – find extremely disturbing, since if it is true, all women run the risk of finding themselves living with an abuser.

Unfortunately, it *is* true. Of course some men who batter their partners are indeed clinically sick, but the majority are not. Many are highly respected, competent, perfectly sane figures, such as judges, clergymen and doctors. Research shows that the proportion of abusers who are mentally unbalanced is no higher than in society as a whole. Furthermore, if these men are mentally ill, why don't they abuse their employers, or strangers in the street? Why is it only their partners, or occasionally a relative who is so close to the woman as to be seen almost as an extension of her?

Furthermore, there are many men who are clinically sick, impotent or socially inadequate and who do not abuse women.

'He has criminal tendencies anyway'

Some men who abuse their partners have histories of violence or criminal records. The majority do not.

'He must be drunk/on drugs'

It is true that some men who abuse their partners are drug-takers or alcoholics. But most are not.

Many of the women I talk to live with men who drink too much and then assault them, but they also assault them when they are sober. Women tell me they take extra precautions if they know their men have been drinking, because they know it gives them an excuse to be more aggressive. But the alcohol is not the root cause.

Blaming drink or drugs is a way of denying responsibility

by pleading loss of control. It is easy for a man to say, 'I was out of control – I was drunk,' or 'I don't remember – I was high at the time,' and society will accept the excuse. But such a man is in control enough to hit only his partner – not others – and he is usually in control enough to stop short of killing the woman.

Most men who batter their wives do not have drink problems at all, and have never taken drugs. Conversely, many men drink too much or take drugs, but would never abuse their partners.

Blaming drink or drugs is simply an excuse. It dodges the real issue. After all, if abuse is simply a product of alcohol or drugs, why don't women who drink or take drugs batter men in equal numbers?

'He was just jealous'

As we have seen, Charm Syndrome Man is usually very jealous indeed – but we must remind ourselves why he is jealous. He is jealous because he cannot bear the idea of losing *control*. He sees his partner as a possession, and no one but him must get close to her. Many men see it as macho to behave in this fashion. People frequently say, 'He's jealous because he's insecure' – and this is partly true. He *is* insecure, because he is frightened of losing his 'possession'. Besides, many men are insecure and jealous, yet they do not feel entitled to abuse their partners because of it.

Jealousy is only one facet of an abuser's controlling behaviour, but it is one of the excuses most readily accepted by abused women and society – and because of its romantic implications it is the one most easily exploited by Charm Syndrome Man. Invariably *he* ends up with the sympathy – not the woman, whose partner interrogates her until the early hours, forbids her to see her friends, or beats her senseless for some imagined misdemeanour.

Jealousy may be a contributory factor in the abuse of women, certainly, but it is not the root cause.

'They just have unmet dependency needs'

Many psychologists argue that both the abuser and his partner are dependent on each other. This dependency is created at infancy, when the child is nourished, encouraged, loved and protected by its mother, and feels panicky and insecure when ignored. For both men and women, the argument goes, this need for someone to fill the mother role lingers in adulthood, so that they both believe they cannot survive without each other, they rely on each other to fulfil every emotional need. When an abusive man believes that his partner is not satisfying these needs, or fears that she might be about to abandon him, he becomes violent or emotionally abusive, while the woman, in her belief that they are vital to each other, feels she cannot leave.

I am not dismissing this theory, but it is only a part of the picture. Many people have 'unmet dependency needs', but they do not become abusers, or find themselves living with abusers. Instead they may withdraw, or eat too much, under-perform at work or become workaholics.

The theory is flawed – because if all babies are brought up with these needs, why is it only the males who become abusers? And the theory fails to take into account the social pressures and lack of facilities which prevent women from leaving their abusers. Nor does it encompass any of the ways in which men are encouraged to batter and abuse by a society which does not take them to task. And if all men and women have these dependency needs, why is it only some men abuse, that only some women are abused? And what about the influence of fathers?

'He is under stress'

I hear this one over and over again. Even in my work training the police, I have come up against a theory that many police officers batter their wives because their job is so stressful. Certainly some men who abuse their wives are suffering from stress but, again, this is an excuse, not a cause. Many men who are stressed do not abuse their wives: similarly, many men who abuse their wives cannot claim to be under stress.

Women also suffer from stress. They may have jobs which demand a great deal of responsibility and decision-making, they too may be made redundant, or they may be trying to care for elderly relatives or look after their family, with an abusive and controlling husband who beats them and refuses to give them money for the housekeeping – yet women rarely beat or abuse their partners to the extent that men abuse women. Stress is simply a red herring.

'He just loses his temper sometimes'

Many people argue that an abusive man merely loses his temper. He is out of control, or, as Deborah Sinclair suggests in *Understanding Wife Assault*, he has 'poor impulse control', he is a 'walking time-bomb' which suddenly explodes.

I would argue that, on the contrary, consciously or subconsciously, an abuser is very much in control. You have only to listen to the stories of abused women to realise that these men are very selective in their violence. Hazel told me that even when Jimmy was trying to choke her, 'He seemed out of control in one way, but there was something controlling this "out of control" part. Even when he appeared to be acting wildly, he was aware of what he was doing.'

Like many abusers, he rarely left marks on prominent parts of her body, since that would attract the attention of friends and neighbours. 'When we were first married,' she noted, 'he broke my nose twice, but later on he started hitting me on the body, because it didn't show. When he hit my face, it got marked, and I lost a lot of jobs because I couldn't show up with my face all marked. So after a while he learned that I couldn't go to work if my face was marked.' Jimmy was no fool: he was unemployed, and his wife was the sole wage-earner.

Laura, too, noticed that her husband learned by his mistakes, and she was frightened that his violence could be so calculated. 'In the beginning,' she says, echoing Hazel's story, 'the first times he hit me, it was a regular black eye, but after that I'm quite sure he took care that it wasn't anywhere that was going to show. I always felt that it was controlled too; and that he could, if he wanted to, hurt me much more. He hit me enough for it to hurt, but not to show; which is pretty frightening, because it's a controlled kind of violence, rather than saying he was drunk out of his head and didn't know what he was doing.'

James was selective about when and where he hit Laura – until the last time. 'He would hit me behind a closed door at the bottom of the house so the children wouldn't wake up,' she says. 'He knew that, if the children ever became involved, that would give me the strength to leave.' On one occasion, he even stopped hitting her, telling her to make a cup of tea, then started again once he had drunk it.

Abusive men are also selective in that they will destroy a woman's possessions, but not their own. They will not smash the television if they enjoy watching it. They do not beat up their bosses or people they hold in high esteem and do not want to alienate – because that would not be to their advantage.

Immediately after an abuser has acted violently towards his partner, or if he is interrupted during his assault, he is frequently able to turn on the charm to convince neighbours, friends and police that the woman is exaggerating things – that he would not dream of laying a finger on her. Does this sound like a man who is out of control?

Experiments show that anger is something which *can* be controlled. If you were to make somebody stand on the edge of a cliff and say to them, 'If you lose your temper, I'll push you off,' then that person would almost certainly manage to keep control. The same is true of abusive men. They *choose* to use their temper as a controlling device. Some are ice cool in planning their attacks, and are therefore particularly frightening. Others less so. Yet even an abuser who seems to be out of control and acting in an explosive rage is prompted by a fundamental need to control. It is that need, however unconscious, which triggers off the violence.

Finally, the fact that many men effectively abuse their partners emotionally and psychologically, without using anger or physical violence at all, surely shows just how much they are in control of the situation.

'It is all a matter of low self-esteem'

Many abusers have low self-esteem. They do not feel good about themselves. They wish they were different. And because they feel so insecure they often adopt another 'image'. Their fears and emotions are masked by controlling, abusive behaviour. They will mock their partners, put them down and lash out at them with fists and words. They convince themselves of their own importance and feel justified in keeping their women in check.

In reality, however, these men are dependent on their partners for this sense of power and superiority. They feel inadequate and worthless, but they cannot admit it. Often, too, they are frightened of real intimacy. The only relationships they can have are ones in which they feel they call all the shots.

However, the issue of men's low self-esteem is only a factor in woman abuse, not the root cause. This is underlined by the fact that many men have low-esteem, but do not abuse their partners, and although both men and women experience feelings of worthlessness and insecurity, only a tiny proportion of women abuse men. When a woman feels insecure and dependent, she does not behave in the same way. Also, there are many men who have low self-esteem, but never abuse their wives and girlfriends – so there must be some other cause.

Many people also argue that only women who have low self-esteem can be abused, but I dispute this. It is true that abusers often seek out women who are lacking in self-esteem, because they are easier to dominate. It is also true that women have inherited a tradition which brands them inferior to men. They live in a society in which their self-esteem is not fostered. I would argue that for most abused women low self-esteem is a *consequence* of the abuse, not a cause. Many women start out in a relationship with high self-esteem, which is systematically broken when the men they fall in love with humiliate, hit and undermine them. However confident and comfortable with themselves they may once have been, they now begin to believe it when their abusers tell them that they are bad or crazy or that it is their fault that the men behave the way they do.

The danger of this particular myth is that once again it focuses the problem on the women. But the problem does not lie with the women – whether they have high self-esteem or low self-esteem. It lies with men and the society in which they live. We have to ask the question: Will boosting a woman's self-esteem stop her partner from being violent? The answer is no. A woman cannot make a man abusive. It is always his choice.

I am not disputing that drink, stress, jealousy, low self-esteem and other such problems can play a part in woman abuse – but I do not accept that they are the cause. Solving any or all of these problems will not end the abuse of women. And concentrating on them only diverts attention from the real issue, excuses the abusers and perpetuates the abuse. Because for as long as it is convenient to be distracted by myths, no one feels the need to do anything about it.

I believe that the cause of woman abuse is more fundamental. Only by looking at our society and culture as a whole can we answer the question: Why do men abuse women?

5

Why Men Abuse Women

Men Are More Important

The way you see a problem determines what you do about it, so if you see woman abuse as being caused by a man drinking too much, you simply send him to Alcoholics Anonymous. If you think it is about a woman's masochism, you send her to an analyst to delve into her subconscious. If you think a man is suffering from some chemical deficiency, you simply administer the appropriate drugs. Many of these factors, which I discussed in the previous chapter, do contribute to abuse, but they do not *cause* it. Woman abuse is the culmination of certain factors.

Deborah Sinclair in her book *Understanding Wife Assault* suggests that three major elements interlock to perpetuate the problem. First, the psychological experiences of the individual men and women (jealousy, fear of abandonment, low self-esteem, stress – all the psychological theories we looked at in the last chapter). Second, the lack of resources (housing, lack of childcare) and the negative responses of the community to the problem (the failure to prosecute, and the attitude of a society which asks, 'What did you do to make him hit you?', 'It takes two . . . ').

We have looked at these factors in the two previous chapters. In this chapter I am going to concentrate on the third major factor: society's beliefs about and attitudes towards the roles of men and women.

For a long time, Sally was unable to see that Guy's

behaviour had nothing to do with *her*, that she did not cause his behaviour, that nothing she tried would change it. Finally, she was able to accept that she was in no way to blame. Nor could she excuse his behaviour with any of society's myths. It was not because he had occasionally drunk too much, because he was under stress at work, or because he was a jealous person. She began to see that what had really been happening was that Guy had been controlling her in a host of subtle ways. And that the responsibility for what he was doing was his. He had learned to behave that way long before he ever met Sally.

Without any prompting, when she came to see me she would tell me that she had noticed similar behaviour in men all around her. 'My best friend's husband does exactly the same thing,' she would say. 'He's always putting her down.' Or 'I can't believe the way my sister has stopped seeing her friends because her boyfriend wants her to be with him all the time.'

'Why are men like that?' she asked. Women who have come to recognise the controlling patterns of their partner's behaviour ask that question all the time. 'I suppose I always thought in terms of men being somehow in charge, but I never thought it was relevant to what was happening to me,' says Rebecca.

I suggested to Sally and Rebecca that the answer to the question 'Why are men like that?' is that they are simply doing on an individual level what men do on a larger scale. The way Guy and Ralph had treated them was just a reflection of the way men treat women in society as a whole. When Guy was grudging about allowing Sally money, he was echoing a society which allows women to earn only 60–69 per cent of the amount that men earn, in spite of equal-pay legislation. When Ralph isolated Rebecca from her friends by turning down invitations and trying to stop her from working, he was behaving the way men behave to women on a much bigger scale, by expecting them to stay at home with their children, forcing them to curtail their social activities and trapping them inside their houses.

When James humiliated and degraded Laura by putting her down in front of their friends and subjecting her to the kind of sexual abuse which made her feel ashamed and unclean, he was just doing what men do on a larger scale: putting them down through the kind of advertising which uses women as 'objects' to sell cars or cocktails, and degrading them through pornography and rape.

'So what?' you might say. 'What has men using women's bodies to sell cars got to do with woman abuse?' People say to me all the time: 'That is just feminist gobbledegook.' But it is not just gobbledegook. There really is a very strong link between the way men treat women in society and the way they abuse them in the home. If men do not respect women on a universal level, there will always be some men who will treat their wives and girlfriends with the same contempt.

'But men and women are equal these days,' people say. 'The women in my office earn just as much as me,' men insist. 'My wife and I have a perfectly equal relationship. We take all the decisions together,' they say. 'I have a woman boss,' they argue. But does that woman boss have a husband who is at home ironing her clothes, cooking her evening meal and looking after the children – or does she come home from work and do it herself?

Okay, so women like Emmeline Pankhurst no longer have to chain themselves to railings, but if it is really true that men and women are equal, how come men still get off scot-free when they bruise and batter their wives? And, more to the point, why have I found myself talking to 3000 abused women who have suffered horrifying emotional and physical scars at the hands of men? Why is it that so many women are afraid to be themselves, to have their own friends, to express their opinions? Why do they spend their lives avoiding anything which might upset their partners, for fear of retribution?

Frankly the idea that men and women are equal is rapidly becoming the myth of the 1990s. The reality is that men and women are not equal. Men are still seen to be superior, and women are still discriminated against. The bottom line is that men have the power and the control, and women are denied it. When one sex is given all the power and control, it is inevitable that there will be some men who will abuse it, and feel entitled to keep their wives and girlfriends in line, even if that means using abusive behaviour to get their own way.

What I hope to show in this chapter is that, however far we think we have come, very little has changed since St Paul wrote in a letter to the Corinthians that the man 'is the image and glory of God, but the woman is the glory of the man'. In too many cases, woman abuse is only a short step away.

In his book *Princess*, Robert Lacey talked of the marriage of Lady Diana Spencer to Prince Charles in terms of a fairy tale, in which Diana fell in love with her prince, the world rejoiced and even the Archbishop of Canterbury talked about fairy tales. They were bound to live happily ever after . . . This is story-book stuff, the kind of orange-blossom ideal we are all brought up on: marriage will bring ultimate happiness; everything else is unimportant. Once you have a ring on your finger, that is it: happy ever after.

Melinda, like many of the women I meet, had been brought up on these ideals. 'I suppose I was looking for the special kind of love my mother and father shared. They really are made for each other,' she explained. 'It's a marriage made in heaven. I had a career, and I had my own home, but I always thought that if I got married, then I'd have what they had. And I thought it would be a happily-ever-after type of thing.'

However, far from the hearts and flowers ideal, the reality of marriage for women frequently turns out to be something entirely different. Charlotte Fedders (see pages 9 and 134) could not believe her luck when she met and married her lawyer husband John. She did not really believe that she deserved such a wonderful man. Fedders, on the other hand, saw in Charlotte someone who would bow down to his every wish, without questioning, someone who accepted that she was in no way his equal.

Nowhere is the idea that men are the dominant sex more clearly expressed than in the institution of marriage. 'Who giveth this woman?' the priest asks in the traditional Church of England wedding service, before going on to demand that she 'love, honour and obey' her husband. 'The day I married Ralph,' says Rebecca, 'I never thought twice about saying those words. In fact I was proud to say them. I never dreamt how literally Ralph would take them. And how much misery it would all mean for me.'

To love, honour and obey – the words sound noble but, for many women whose men hold such beliefs, abuse is only a step away. 'I think I became James's property after we got married,' says Laura, looking back. 'I don't think I was before. And I hadn't reckoned on that, because that's not how I think about things at all.' Hazel says, 'The day Jimmy and I got married, he said to me: "You are my property now," and that made me uneasy. Just for a moment, I thought, "God, what have I done? I am *his*."' The brief niggle vanished, because she was convinced she was going to live happily ever after.

And, as we have seen, it is not only married women who are in danger. Charm Syndrome Man is looking for commitment, but there need not be a wedding ring involved. Sally says, 'Guy and I weren't married, but we might as well have been. All that was missing was the piece of paper. If we had got married, I doubt if I would have promised to love honour and obey – but it wouldn't have made any difference to his attitude. I think that's the way he expected me to behave, anyway.'

Before the then Sarah Ferguson married Prince Andrew, she announced in a TV interview: 'When we are in a dilemma or situation which needs someone to make a decision it will be Andrew who will take the lead. He will make the decision because he is the man of the marriage. Therefore, in that sense, I will obey him at one stage or another.' Many women agree with the Duchess of York's views and live happily ever after. But many do not, because although such views seem perfectly normal and comfortable these conventional attitudes actually sow the seeds of woman abuse. We are totally steeped in the tradition of men being the dominant sex. They are the ones who take charge and fight wars. They are the heads of families, the breadwinners. But these very attitudes give men the power and control which can be so dangerous. So when people ask, 'Why do men abuse women?', one answer is simply, 'Because they always have done.'

The Charm Syndrome is a term I have invented, but the behaviour it describes is as old as civilisation. Historically women have always been regarded as chattels to be handed over in marriage. But we have come a long way since the days when men 'owned' their women like goods and chattels, I hear you say. But have we? When Pamela, the eponymous heroine of Samuel Richardson's eighteenth-century novel, speaks about 'Mr. B's rules for marriage' I hear Rebecca talking about Ralph, or Melinda talking about Trevor. The language is different, but the sentiments are remarkably similar.

Says Pamela:

> I must think his displeasure the heaviest thing that can befall me. And so, that I must not wish to incur it, to save my body else from it, I must bear with him, even when I find him in the wrong. He insists upon it, that a woman should give her husband reason to think she prefers him before all men.
>
> If she overcomes, he says, it must be by sweetness and compliance. She must not shew reluctance, uneasiness or doubt, in obliging him; and that too at half a word, and must not be bidden twice to do one thing. In all companies a wife must shew respect and love to her husband.

By giving men the dominant role, the institution of marriage still denies women real choices. Women are still trapped by marriage. They sacrifice their careers to raise children, and in doing so they often become financially dependent on their partners, and isolated from the outside interests, stimulation and relationships which working in a job can bring. They often deny their own talents, by supporting their husbands while they go through further education. Many women tell me that they have taken menial jobs in order to pay for their husbands to go to law school or medical school. Often in these cases, the men walk out on them, and the women are left with boring jobs and no money, while the men start new lives on a high income, thanks to the women's sacrifices.

Even when women have jobs outside the home, they still do the lion's share of the housework, catering to their partner's specific needs at the expense of their own. They are expected to be Superwomen, juggling job and home. At the same time they must never neglect their partner's emotional needs. Frequently such women find themselves exhausted from doing half a dozen jobs, while the men only have to concentrate on one.

Society teaches women that their role is to look after home and family, to be the emotional ballast. Men, on the other hand, are the breadwinners, the decision-makers, the heads of the family. 'Wait till your father gets home' is the threat that many children grow up with, and never shake off. Rebecca laughingly admits that she used to bounce on the sofa with the children while Ralph was away – because he forbade her to even sit on it.

Charm Syndrome Man sees his partner as the rightful object of his authority. He believes he can control her actions, even her thoughts. And even when his behaviour becomes intolerable, she is trapped into staying in the relationship because society says she must. 'For the sake of the children,' people say, or 'It's up to you to make it work.'

No matter how 'equal' women think they are, no matter how strong they may appear to others or how many crucial decisions they may make at work every day, women have been so brainwashed with the idea that their happiness is tied up with pleasing their partners and creating the 'perfect' home that they are rarely able to reject the notion. If they do so, they risk being branded 'ranting feminists'.

The result of such brainwashing is that it widens even further the gulf between men and women in terms of power. He goes on thinking he is superior, that he has the power to treat his partner in any way he thinks is right, while she believes it is her responsibility to make things work. In such an unequal partnership it is inevitable that some men are always going to resort to violence and abuse to enforce their superiority.

So Men Call All the Shots

As I have pointed out, men abuse women because they are allowed to do so – and have always been allowed to do so. For as long as men have considered that a woman's life revolves around her man, that her role is to love, honour and obey him – for better or for worse – there have been secular laws and moral codes which have given men the go-ahead to underline that idea with abuse. And even in this so-called enlightened age, when such barbaric laws have been abolished (at least in this country), the thinking behind them still prevails.

The history books are peppered with codes and laws which enforce the idea that, if women do not behave as men think they should, they can be punished. As long ago as 2500 BC, if a woman argued with her husband, her name was engraved on a brick which was then used to smash out her teeth.

In the fifteenth century, one Friar Cherubino of Siena produced a volume called *The Rules of Marriage*. He instructed: 'When you see your wife commit an offence, don't rush at her with insults and violent blows; rather, first correct the wrong lovingly and pleasantly, and sweetly teach her not to do it again so as not to offend God, injure her soul, or bring shame upon herself or you . . . ' However, if that does not work, he advises, 'Scold her sharply, bully and terrify her.'

And if *that* is not enough, 'Take a stick and beat her soundly
. . . not in rage, but out of charity and concern for her
soul, so that the beating will rebound to your merit and
her good.'

The Koran gives a similar message: 'Men are the managers of the affairs of women. Righteous women are therefore
obedient and those you fear may be rebellious admonish.
Banish them to their couches and beat them.'

The idea that men were entitled to chastise their wives
was echoed in secular law. Even in the relatively civilised
era of Charles I, it was accepted that a man could beat his
wife – but not after dark, as that might disturb the peace.

Most people have heard the phrase 'rule of thumb', but
not so many know that it refers to the common law tradition
that allowed a man to chastise his wife, so long as it was
with a stick no thicker than his thumb – and that is about
the size of a broomstick!

Things seemed to be looking up in 1861, when the
Offences Against the Person Act made assault a crime.
Surely now women would be safe? Not so. Only eight years
later the philosopher John Stuart Mill wrote,

> From the earliest twilight of human society, every
> woman . . . was found in a state of bondage to some
> man. How vast is the number of men in any great
> country, who are little higher than brutes, and . . . this
> never prevents them from being able, through the laws
> of marriage, to obtain a victim . . .
>
> The vilest malefactor has some wretched woman tied
> to him, against whom he can commit any atrocity except killing her . . . and even that he can do without
> too much danger of legal penalty.

And in 1878 Frances Power Cobbe published a report called
Wife Torture in England. She asked, 'What reasons can be
alleged . . . why the male of the human species should be
the only animal which maltreats its mate, or any female
of its own kind?'

That is a very good question – to which the only answer can be: man is the only animal brought up in a society which encourages him to behave in such a way, and then turns a blind eye. Today, men still assault women – because rarely does anyone stop them from doing so. Even though the law in theory offers protection, in practice it fails to provide it. In the majority of cases the police still do not arrest and charge offenders, and Crown Prosecutors are reluctant to prosecute.

Our society has not really changed so much since the twelfth century, when the monk Gratian decreed, 'It is a natural human order that women should serve their husbands.'

As Hazel's parish priest advised her whenever she turned to him for help, 'Marriage is a sacred thing. I know it can be difficult at times, but it is your duty to love your husband and look after him.' Another cleric advised a woman who had been attacked by her husband with a hammer and chisel to do the same thing. He told her he would make her husband swear on the Bible never to do it again, and then she should go home to him. Six months later she turned up at the Refuge with further injuries.

When I asked Sally about her background and her life before she met Guy, she told me, 'I had always been brought up with the idea that I was nothing without a man, that having a career was all well and good, but not at the expense of a husband and family.' The more I asked women the same question, the more I became convinced that no matter how high-powered their jobs, no matter how intelligent or well-off the women were, they were all brought up to think that their ultimate happiness depended on a man.

Hazel says, 'I think what I was looking for subconsciously when I met Jimmy was a man, a husband, to protect me and be a father to my children. I didn't want much – I didn't want to be rich, to have power, or to be famous. I didn't want a fancy car, or a lot of material possessions. I really didn't expect much. I just wanted a man, a house and two kids. That was what I was looking for. And Jimmy was lovely, he was gorgeous. There I was thinking, "I've got what I wanted." Of course it wasn't to be . . . '

Finding a man who has a good job, is reliable and makes a nice income is also seen to be a kind of status symbol. Telling the story of Charlotte Fedders and her husband John in *Shattered Dreams*, Laura Elliott writes: 'On the outside John was the knight that she and her affluent, Catholic school girlfriends had been taught to want – the handsome, ambitious breadwinner, through whom they could vicariously be successes.' Charlotte's upbringing had led her to place an enormous emphasis on this idea of achieving status through a man who could support her.

Despite shouts of 'Men and women are equal these days!' women are still trained to be dependent, to believe that they are unable to stand on their own feet, and that they have to rely on men for protection, stability and support. Women who are dependent have less power. They feel unable to challenge what they have been conditioned to think is the norm. They do not believe they have rights. Nor do men – who have of course absorbed the same message. As long as women are trapped in this way, men will always exploit them.

Both men and women search for that certain someone and that certain chemistry which sets pulses racing, making them feel special, important, fulfilled. Both men and women sing love songs and write love poetry. Yet for women there is this extra emphasis, that without a man they are nothing.

Women are brought up with the warning, 'You don't want to be left on the shelf, dear,' ringing in their ears. What a cruel expression, with its connotation of goods no one wants. In just the same way, the word 'spinster' has acquired connotations of someone old and wizened and prim, with no experience of men – but call an unmarried man a 'bachelor' and the automatic image is of someone handsome, eligible, a 'bit of a rogue' with women.

When men fall in love it tends to be only a part of their life, rather than an all-consuming thing. Their careers are equally, often more, important. For women the opposite is usually true. As Lord Byron wrote in *Don Juan*:

> Man's love is of man's life a thing apart,
> 'Tis woman's whole existence.

The result is a dangerous inequality between the sexes.

As I explained to Sally and Rebecca, the controlling behaviour they suffered at the hands of Guy and Ralph were only symptoms of a much wider problem. The way abusive men behave towards their partners is magnified on a much larger scale in society as a whole. And women are no more responsible for that than they are in their individual relationships.

When people insist that men and women are equal these days, I say, 'Look around you.' It simply is not true. 'But we have a woman Prime Minister,' people insist. I answer, how many women MPs are there? The answer is 42, compared to 650 men. In key positions in the country men also have the monopoly. It is very easy to say glibly, 'Times have changed – we have a Sex Discrimination Act,' and point out that there are women pilots, engineers, roadsweepers. But these are almost always 'token' women. The advances are not across the board.

In England and Wales, in the medical profession there are 21,053 male GPs and 5456 women GPs. There are 793 male gynaecologists, compared with 92 women, 1295 male consultants and only 60 women. In the same area there are only 16 female judges, and 383 men. There are 45,000 male solicitors and 8000 females. There are 610 male QCs, and 30 women. As far as accountants are concerned, 82,125 of them are men, 8781 women. And the fact that a female can study sciences and engineering at university, or pilot a commercial aircraft, has not changed the fundamental idea lodged in many people's minds, that men are the leaders, the dominant sex who have inherited the right to exert power over women.

Not only are women discriminated against in the work-place, but they are disadvantaged in other ways. Nine out of ten single parents are women. Statistics from the National Council for One-Parent Families show that most of these families are living in poverty, with inadequate amenities, such as telephones, transport, even heating. Remarkably, women in Britain were allowed to take charge of their own income tax affairs through separate taxation only in 1990.

There are fewer women undergraduates in UK universities, fewer apprenticeships and day-release courses available for women. Studies have shown that in schools boys receive more attention than girls. In *Gender and Schooling* Michelle Stanworth writes, 'Girls may follow the same curriculum as boys – may sit side by side with boys in classes taught by the same teachers – and yet emerge from school with the implicit understanding that the world is a man's world, in which women can and should take second place.'

The point is that in schools, where boys and girls receive some of the strongest messages about their roles in life, they are still being taught that men get the most important jobs, that they make the decisions, that, in general, they are superior. Women, on the other hand, have fewer choices, because their future is not simply tied up with a career – they have marriage and children to think about. Planning for a long-term future is not high on a girl's list of priorities, because for both pupil and teacher the attitude is 'Well, I expect you'll get married and have children.'

The same attitude is evident when women go for job interviews. Men are still reluctant to give women jobs which involve long-term planning and commitment because they expect them to abandon their work to have children. I hear stories all the time of women not being offered contracts, or partnerships, for this reason – however insistent the women are that they are singleminded about their jobs and have no intention of having children at that time. Men and women have been saturated with these ideas for so long that, however enlightened we may think we are, we are still locked into the idea that men are entitled to be in charge.

Women are barely less discriminated against than they were between the fifteenth and eighteenth centuries when some nine million women in Europe and America were stigmatised as witches and burned at the stake, because they challenged men's authority by running their estates and businesses when their husbands were at war or had died of plague. Other women who challenged the monopoly of male physicians by using country remedies for healing met the same fate.

Have we really made such great strides since the days when women were denied the vote, when they had to adopt male pseudonyms to write their novels because otherwise they laid themselves open to accusations of neglecting their husbands and families? Are we really any more inclined to see the world as a place where women are important any more than we did when our only view of history was coloured by men and their attitudes and beliefs, male explorers, male scientists, male composers, male writers giving us *their* view of the world? Where are the women? Names like Elizabeth Browning and Emmeline Pankhurst are exceptions, they are not the rule.

Women may be referred to as 'the power behind the throne' but that expression makes them even more invisible. Many women have had to fulfil their own ambitions through their sons or their husbands because they have not been allowed to do so themselves. The woman's role is to nurture her men towards power and success. The man is the one who gets all the credit and all the glory.

In all sorts of subtle ways, all these historical references are more stitches in the tapestry of woman abuse. Men believe they have the right to control and dominate women because they have historically been given that right. We are saturated with the idea that men call the shots. Women say to me all the time 'I prefer the company of men to women,' or 'I'd rather work with men than women' – what they are really saying is that men, to them, are more important, so they want to be associated with them rather than with women, whom they see (probably unconsciously) as inferior. So long as women feel this way, and so long as they either do not see that men call all the shots or do not think it matters, they can never be united in helping each other to change things.

Just as individual women tend to deny what is happening to them, because facing up to it means taking difficult and often painful decisions, women as a whole do the same thing. It is easier to deny reality by accepting the traditional notion that men are supposed to be in charge. The idea is so ingrained that we do not even notice it half the time – but it is there and, as long as it is there, so is the problem of woman abuse.

And Women Get the Bit Parts

From an early age, women are taught that men are important and women get the bit parts. In children's books it is Mother Bear who wears the pinny and makes the cakes, while Father Bear goes out to work. Mothers in children's stories rarely do or say anything challenging. They are never seen making important decisions. They simply make the sandwiches for picnics, cook the supper and wash the clothes.

One American study of children's literature (*Sex Role Socialization in Picture Books for Preschool Children*) found that female characters were outnumbered by male characters three to one. Even when stories were about animals they tended to be male. Females played menial, supporting roles, while the male characters had all the adventures. As the survey noted, 'It is easy to imagine that the little girl reading these books might be deprived of her ego and her sense of self. She may be made to feel that girls are vacuous creatures who are less worthy and do less exciting things than men.'

In her book *A Woman's Place: The Changing Picture of Women in Britain*, Diana Souhami notes that in a children's ABC published by Abelard-Schuman in 1980, which illustrated each letter of the alphabet with a picture of someone doing a job, women get only five out of the twenty-six jobs. She also remarks that research by Geoffrey Walford in 1980 found that in physics textbooks used in schools, 80 per cent of the illustrations showed only men, 8 per cent showed both sexes and 12 per cent showed a woman or girl alone, and these appeared 'in a bathing suit, in a bath, as a nurse, with a vacuum cleaner . . . much more often than they appear as active participants in experiments or a physics-related production'.

Despite a vogue for adverts and magazines aimed at the career woman, the advertiser's favourite image of a woman is still either the temptress draped over a sleek, sexy new car, the housewife fretting over how she can get little Johnny's sports shirt clean for the morning, or how many dinner services she can wash up with a particular brand of liquid. Men, on the other hand, discuss the finer points of desk-top publishing while they jet across the Atlantic on business, or wax lyrical about their favourite pint of bitter in the pub, leaving their wives at home. The result of such stereotyping is that neither men nor women have real choices about their roles.

Why should it be so tough for women to be the higher wage-earners and higher achievers in a relationship – *if* they want to be; and why do men so often fear ridicule if they express their vulnerability? Of course I am not suggesting that all women should go out to work and all men should stay at home and be with the children – the point is that they should be free to choose whichever role suits them best. If a woman decides to stay at home and enjoys bringing up her children, it should be because that is what she wants. She should not feel trapped in a role which is expected of her. Nor should men feel trapped in the role of breadwinner.

They should be free to hand that over to their partner if that is what makes them both happy. Yet the truth is that men's jobs are always given more status; even single fathers get more praise and attention than single mothers.

If women attempt to change their role, society has a way of putting them down through sharp language. Women who try to be different are frequently branded 'butch', 'lesbians' or 'spinsters' – all words which are loaded with contempt. Men who try to change their own roles are too often considered 'weak', 'effeminate' or 'namby-pamby'. A society which baulks at changing the traditional roles of men and women, however much it may protest otherwise, also perpetuates the kind of extremism which results in the abuse of women.

Another way in which men are able to maintain control over women is by devaluing them in all kinds of ways: on television, in pornography and through prostitution, in advertising which uses women in sexy attire to sell sports cars, and in newspapers and magazines. Whenever a woman is draped naked over the centrefold of a men's magazine, the message is that women are there simply to titillate men. If women are cheapened and treated as objects, is it any wonder that in their individual relationships men feel entitled to treat them badly?

Pornography is not sexy or erotic. Pornography is about degrading women and portraying them as servile, sexual objects, with a status which is little higher than that of an animal. Often such 'titillation' is linked with violence: women are shown in bondage or being mutilated. Extraordinarily enough, a recent display in the window of a shop selling women's fashions showed the 'dummies' with cuts, bruises and bandages, and their hands bound behind their backs. On a less blatant level, whenever a woman is called a 'chick', a 'bit of fluff' or a 'bird', or is whistled at from a building site, the message she receives is that she is not a person, but an object of men's sexual fantasies.

Pornography, rape and sexual harassment serve as reminders of the threat that always hangs over women.

Because they are unable to walk the streets freely, because they are told they should not wear 'provocative' clothing, or say things which could be construed as encouraging men to 'take advantage' of them, they are isolated, their social lives are curtailed, they are denied the same freedom that men have. Ironically, women are taught that they need male protection against these very things. Rape is more than a violent crime – it underlines the lack of respect with which men treat women. One of the earliest laws on rape is to be found in the Book of Deuteronomy: 'If a man find a damsel that is a virgin, that is not betrothed, and lay hold on her, and lie with her, and they be found: then the man that lay with her shall give unto the damsel's father fifty shekels of silver, and she shall be his wife . . . ' In other words, the father gets compensation for damaged goods and the daughter's 'compensation' is marriage to the rapist.

'But that was a long time ago,' people will say. So it was, but the attitudes it illustrates have changed very little. After all, rape within marriage is still legal, and men do not always receive stiff punishment for rape. Even nowadays, they can be let off by a judge deciding that the woman deserved it because she wore a mini skirt or walked down a dark road late at night.

From the cradle almost, men and women are brought up to see their roles in life as different: he is dominant, she is dependent. There is no escaping the fact that little girls are brought up differently from little boys.

Boys frequently grow up sneering at displays of emotion or at gentle pastimes, for fear of being considered 'soft' or 'sissies'. They are brought up to be tough, to play with guns and tanks and dumper trucks, and show their aggression on the football pitch and the rugby field. They are taught that boys should take control, be forceful, be dominant. Aggressive play is too often considered healthy in a little boy.

Girls, on the other hand, are encouraged to be sweet, affectionate and compliant. They are taught that girls should be self-sacrificing and caring. They are dressed up like little dolls in frothy outfits which stop them from

expressing themselves in the rough and tumble world of
their brothers, and they are given dolls' houses and ironing
boards and toy vacuum cleaners.

As Linda Tschirhart Sanford and Mary Ellen Donovan
note in *Women and Self-Esteem*, 'Boys are encouraged to
fight back when others try to violate them, and as a result
many males unfortunately see violence as the normal way
to try to resolve a variety of problems. Girls, however,
are encouraged to do nothing, and the helplessness a
girl learned in childhood often carries over into adulthood, where passivity seems the only way to handle
problems. . . . ' Little girls who grow up absorbing such
attitudes expect few choices to be available to them. They
expect to be 'given away' in marriage, and to become the
property of their husbands. Little boys grow up expecting
their partners to be subordinate to them.

The idea that men are the important, dominant sex, on
whom women depend for their happiness, is reinforced
in the story books which play such an important part in
forming children's attitudes. Little girls grow up with the
image of the Lady in all those knight-in-shining-armour
epics, or the Sleeping Beauty, the beautiful maiden who can
only be brought to life by her handsome prince. Instead
of helping herself, Sleeping Beauty has to wait passively
to be rescued. The myth – set up by the male writers
of such books and supported by a society which has been
advocating such ideas for centuries – is that women are
helpless, passive, servile creatures who cannot think for
themselves, while the men have the important, active roles.
Consequently women grow up with the idea that they do
not have power and control over their own lives. And men
grow up with the idea that women are powerless creatures
simply waiting to be turned on by them.

The knight in shining armour was the champion of God
crusading through Europe, waging war on infidels and (in
the tradition of courtly love) wooing beautiful, submissive
and untouchable women from afar. But since the whole
ethos of courtly love depended on the fact that the knight

conducted his courtship of his lady by remote control, there was no question of any kind of real relationship. The woman was simply a symbol, an object through which the knight could show off his valour and gallantry.

For the woman's part, the knight in shining armour became the romantic ideal: but what did he really represent? A charming but domineering character who took all the initiatives and believed in using violence to enforce his beliefs. Where have we heard that before?

When the little girl grows up she receives the same messages from popular songs and novels. In a current hit London musical, the heroine sings dreamily of the power her hero has to move her, to change, mould and *improve* her. The words suggest that both the heroine and hero assume that *he* has the right to fashion *her* in any way he pleases. Boys too are susceptible to the message in such lyrics.

A similar idea is perpetuated in the Mills and Boon-style romantic novel. It is true that a whole new wave of best-selling novels, soap operas and television mini-series has spawned a different kind of heroine: the independent, glamorous woman who claws her way to the top of a business empire by her perfectly manicured fingernails, giving every male in sight hell on the way. But it is the novelty of the idea which gives it such instant appeal. And such dramas invariably conclude with the woman realising that her work is meaningless without the love of a good man – invariably a hero tough enough and powerful enough not to take no for an answer, even from her. In rejecting the weak characters she meets along the way, in favour of the strong man who takes control, this kind of heroine is still reinforcing the traditional idea that men should take the dominant role. If a woman is strong and capable, it simply requires an even stronger, even more powerful man to take her in hand.

Throughout our culture the idea that a woman might have potential is pushed to one side. The lesson is: men should be looking for women who will fulfil all their needs, while they go out into the big wide world and develop their potential: women should be searching for the Prince Charming who will sweep her off to live happily ever after.

I believe that having sowed the seeds of woman abuse, society (albeit tacitly) gives men permission to go on controlling and abusing their partners – by turning a blind eye to the abuse, blaming the women, perpetuating the myths about the causes of abuse and failing to provide adequate care, facilities and, above all, legal protection for women who have suffered at the hands of abusive men.

Of course, not all men who grow up receiving such signals from society go on to abuse women. When all the analysis is done, the truth is that men *always have a choice*. It may be very difficult for them to shake off the messages they have been bombarded with since they were children, but they still have the choice whether or not to abuse women. They can turn away, and take a different course. It is up to society to make them do that. But society cannot do that until it stops shirking the issue and accepts the real cause of woman abuse. Once we can all accept it, we can try to work together to find a way forward.

6

The Way Forward

For Women

'For so long,' says Melinda, 'I carried on rather than face the horror. I couldn't think of myself as abused, because it was just too unacceptable. I couldn't bear to think about it, but now I would say to any woman in that situation: "Ask yourself whether you are going to accept that you've been abused for X number of years, and you can't do anything about it except go. Or whether you are going to ignore it and live the rest of your life caught in this cycle. *The rest of your life.*"'

The first step for an abused woman is to recognise what is happening to her. Suffering in silence not only prolongs the agony, it also gives an abuser tacit permission to continue his behaviour. What is more, remember that where physical violence is involved, it is a crime. And it is particularly important that women who are being emotionally, socially and verbally ill treated by their partners should understand that they are just as abused as women who are attacked with hammers and knives – and, furthermore, they do not have to put up with it.

Five out of the six women who have told of their experiences in this book have left their husbands and boyfriends and, to varying degrees, have begun to rebuild their self-esteem and their lives – often slowly, painfully and with very mixed emotions. But they have all – with help from friends, relations and counsellors – found a way forward.

'Are you abused?'

To all women who feel depressed, trapped, isolated and resentful in their relationships, I would like to say: ask yourself some searching questions.

Are you afraid of your partner? Do you feel you have to change your behaviour to please him – for example, do you avoid challenging him, or doing and saying things which might make him angry? Perhaps you tell white lies to avoid his temper, so that little things such as lying about who you are talking to on the phone become instinctive. Do you appear confident and self-assured at work and with your friends but nervous and afraid to express an opinion when he is around?

Has your partner ever threatened you, or intimidated you by using violent language or smashing up the furniture?

Do you feel you have no hobbies or friends of your own? Does your partner make it difficult for you to see family and friends? Does he expect you to be with *him* all the time? Is he jealous or possessive?

Do you find yourself agreeing with his criticisms of your friends and others? Do you adopt his values and attitudes simply to preserve the peace?

Does he exclude you from his life? Does he seem secretive? Does he find excuses not to take you places such as office parties or to meet his friends and colleagues?

Is he chauvinistic? Does he work all hours, yet insist that no wife of his is going to work? Or if you do work, is he jealous of what you do (irrespective of the fact that the family may rely on the money you earn)? Is he suspicious of your colleagues – does he think they are coming between you and him, or accuse you of having an affair with some-one at work?

Does he insist that the home and the children are your

responsibility, and refuse to help out, even if you both have full-time jobs?

Does he get over-involved in your life, solving all your problems in a seemingly caring way, such as getting your car repaired, filling in your tax forms, sorting out your car insurance, making all your decisions for you – until he has undermined your independence?

Does he frequently humiliate and embarrass you, show you up or put you in the wrong – often in front of family and friends – so that you feel that *he* gets all the sympathy, and *you* are seen in a bad light?

Do you feel that whatever you do you cannot seem to please him – that you cannot seem to win?

Does he constantly bring up past 'misdemeanours' as if he is keeping a mental diary of everything you have done 'wrong' to use against you later? Do you feel as though he is always trying to catch you out?

Does he lie, even about small things? Is he demanding, childish? Is he a perfectionist to the point of being petty about small things?

Does he operate on double standards? Does he, for example, demand that you do everything according to his idea of an orderly, regimented timetable, while himself doing things when he feels like it?

Do you always put him first and yourself last? Do you juggle a job with a family, exhausting yourself in the process, while he pursues outside interests? It may be that this pattern is so ingrained that you put yourself last in the subtlest, most unconscious ways. For example, do you say things like 'He's very good, he lets me go out with my friends once a week.' Think about it – what you are really saying is: he *allows* me to do these things. What he is doing, in fact, is controlling you.

Does he expect you to be his emotional prop, yet fail to give you the same kind of attention, accusing you of being over-emotional or self-centred – when in fact he is being the self-centred one? Have there been times when you have needed understanding and affection – perhaps when a close relative or friend is ill or has died – only to be asked, 'But what about me – I was close to them too' or 'I wish you'd spend as much time worrying about *me*'?

Does he always turn conversations around to centre on himself? Is it always *me, me, me*?

Is he narcissistic? Does he always have to win? To be perfect? Always right? Does he constantly criticise and blame you or others for everything that is wrong in his life, rather than accept that he might have made a mistake?

Is making love a shared, intimate experience, or do you feel that he is simply using your body without any consideration for your feelings?

Do you sometimes doubt your judgement – or even your sanity? Do you feel guilty that you are unhappy? Do you feel that *you* must be to blame if things are going wrong – and does your partner imply that this is the case?

If you leave, or threaten to leave, does he become all charming again and rush back into your life? Does he start telling you how special you are and then when you are attached to him again does he resort to his abusive behaviour?

If a woman recognises her relationship in this checklist, she is being abused – she may not necessarily have bruises to show for it, but emotional abuse can be just as debilitating.

Facing up to the fact that you are abused can be bewildering, confusing and frightening, as Melinda found out. 'When I actually said those words, "I am abused," I felt stupid, as if I had been made a fool of,' she says. 'I was an independent, intelligent person – how could this have happened to me? And why didn't I see it earlier? But one of the best things that counselling did for me was to show me that I wasn't stupid and that Trevor's behaviour was actually nothing to do with me. It was his problem.' It is hard to recognise abuse because Charm Syndrome Man's behaviour changes insidiously. The abuse creeps so gradually into the relationship that often a woman cannot see what is happening.

Women in Melinda's situation have enough to cope with without making things harder by blaming themselves and feeling silly or guilty for having lived with an abusive man. It is just like finding themselves the victims of a hijack – it could happen to anyone. But, unlike hijackings, abusive relationships are both prevalent and kept secret. Their existence, and their extent, needs to be exposed.

When I am counselling women I often use another analogy. I tell them: imagine you are riding a tiger in the jungle. It's dangerous to stay put but, if you get off, the tiger may eat you. So what do you do? It feels as though you are in a no-win situation. But there *is* an alternative. You could try grabbing the branches which are all around you, and pull yourself off, out of his reach. Eventually he will pursue someone else, and you will feel safe and confident enough to plant your feet back on the ground.

It is time to be positive and grab some of those branches: reach out to other people, build your self-esteem, find new interests. Give yourself credit for recognising the situation *now*, and for wanting to do something about it. Rather than waste your strength on negative feelings, you need to congratulate yourself on having coped for so long.

Often it helps to talk to someone who will listen, understand and help.

'Tell someone . . . '

'The first thing to do is talk to somebody you can trust,' says Rebecca. 'I know it's an old cliché, but a problem shared is a problem halved. Coming to Chiswick and having counselling was the turning point for me. So I think it's so important to talk to someone who understands and maybe also has a professional understanding. Having said that,' she admits, 'the hardest thing was telling somebody first of all. When I first rang Chiswick I felt that you would say, "You can't

come here, you're not a battered wife. You're supposed to
have broken bones and things." I really thought that.'

When Rebecca first came to see me, like many women
she did not really think of herself as abused. She only knew
that she was unhappy. Often I ask such women to imagine
what they would say if their best friend came to them and
told them the same story. How would they react if they
discovered that their best friend's partner was abusing her
in all sorts of ways? Wouldn't they tell her that it was not her
fault, that he had no right to behave in that way, that she is
a worthwhile person and does not deserve such treatment?
Often it helps women to distance themselves in this way.
They are able to see things much more clearly if they
imagine their problems as belonging to someone else.

A woman should not feel that if she asks for help she has
failed in her relationship, or that she is betraying her partner
because she cannot take the abuse any more. Keeping her
problems to herself will only help to perpetuate the abuse
– both on an individual level and for women throughout
society.

Talking to the *right* person is important. Though it may be
that a woman will benefit from talking to someone with the
professional skills to show her a way forward, just talking to
a friend can be the first step for many women. Often the first
reaction is going to be disbelief. Be prepared for reactions
like 'I can't believe it – he's so brilliant, so charming' or
'We all thought you were quite happy.' But if such friends
are really going to be supportive, once they have got over
the shock they will listen, believe what a woman says and
not judge or blame her.

However, if they refuse to accept that the man could
behave in this way, if they say things like 'Why don't you
go out and buy a sexy nightie?' or 'Go away for a weekend'
or 'Cook him a candle-lit dinner' (the sort of crass options
suggested in women's magazines in articles with headlines
like 'How To Win Your Man Back'), then a woman needs
to turn to someone else who can be more constructive
– someone who will listen and not blame her, who will

encourage and help her to see that she has options; someone who will understand that she is swimming in a sea of despair, guilt, shame, fear. She herself needs to accept that she has already expended prodigious efforts to make the relationship work – it is not she who needs to change, but her partner.

Opening up about her fears to the right person makes them more manageable, so it becomes easier for her to cope with her anxieties. Just talking about her experiences can make her feel much stronger, less guilty. Once things are out in the open she may be able to see her situation more clearly, to see that her husband or boyfriend has no justification for treating her this way, and that there are alternatives – and people who will help her to achieve them. There are refuges, social workers, the Samaritans, law centres and Citizens' Advice Bureaux, all of whom can point women in the right direction.

It is important for a woman to build up her own supportive network: sympathetic friends, support groups, therapists – whoever she can trust and call upon when she has doubts and fears and her resolve is weakening and she feels tempted to make excuses for her partner. Hazel says, 'I'd advise women in my situation to confide in somebody and go for help. I know it's hard, but they mustn't think they're the only ones it's happened to, they shouldn't feel dirty or unclean. Go for help, because if you don't it doesn't get better. It gets worse. I believe that once somebody has abused you that way for a long time, it won't change. If you want any kind of life, I think you've got to realise that you have to be away from your abuser. Life is too short to live like that. Just talk about it. Tell people.'

Laura was put in a position where she had to tell complete strangers about her situation, but she found that opening up about it in this way can be a good form of therapy. She explains, 'Because James had gone to the children's headmasters and headmistresses and said things like "My wife's crazy, my wife's drunk, and my wife's a drug addict, she's irresponsible and she's thrown me out of the house and is living in an immoral way taking drugs with somebody else," I had to do things like go to them and say, "Look I'm not an alcoholic."

'I had to put my case to these people I'd never met before, and I had to learn to go there, be calm, be me, and say what the facts were, when I was actually trembling and shaking and feeling far less like me than I'd ever felt in my life. And it was very difficult indeed at first. But, gradually, people have got to know me, and they are very supportive to me. But at first I could tell that they were just sort of testing, and that's very tough when you're going through all of that.

'I must say that both the headmaster and the headmistress were wonderful. The minute I said, "Well, actually the problem was that he used to hit me," they were both fantastic. They said, "Well done, you've obviously done the right thing," which was amazing. Had they said, "I don't believe you" it would have been devastating – because there had been a lot of that, mostly from people connected with him and his family, who believed his side of the story and nothing else. And because I had to face that with so many different people in entirely different situations, including courts and solicitors and everything else, it became therapeutic in itself.

'It was like that with friends too. Because they didn't really know the situation – because I had never told them – they would ring up and say, "Look, why have you left him? He's desperate and he's going to commit suicide," and so I'd have to go through the whole story again, and each time a bit more would come out. And it was good to talk about it. It's just the fact of saying, "Look, I've done it. I've walked away. I don't have to put up with it, and I won't." By doing that you can fight your way through.'

'Take your time'

'After I had been to Chiswick and talked to people and finally admitted what was happening, I had an overwhelming feeling of panic,' says Melinda. 'Okay, I had said those words, "I am abused," but now what? I felt that I couldn't stay in the relationship, now that I could see what was going on. But the idea of leaving, of finding somewhere to go, of making all those decisions terrified me. I think that, despite everything, I wasn't ready to leave. The emotional bond with Trevor was still very strong.'

'You have to make your own decision. If somebody tells you you've got to leave, it doesn't help you,' agrees Hazel, who also found the idea of simply packing her bags and walking out on Jimmy for ever too much to face in one fell swoop.

It is very, very important for a woman to make her own decisions in her own time. She should try not to feel overwhelmed by the need to answer the question, 'Should I stay or should I leave?' And well-meaning friends and advisers should never try to force her into leaving. The last thing she wants to do is swap one person who is controlling her life for another friend or relative who appears to be doing the same thing, however well intentioned. It is time for the woman to take her own decisions, to begin to regain control over her *own* life, however slow that process may be.

Many women, who tell me they would like to leave their partner, obviously half hope that there is some pithy formula with almost magical powers which will enable them to walk painlessly away from the relationship. They feel paralysed. But leaving a partner is more of a process than a single decisive act. I always suggest to women trapped in this way that they try asking themselves what is the worst thing that could happen if they leave. Many women say they are afraid of being lonely, or they worry about taking the children away from their father, or they feel that they will not find another man. Sometimes they worry about managing financially. Then I suggest they ask themselves if these fears outweigh the misery of staying. Perhaps there are other alternatives they haven't considered.

Look at your life as impersonally as you can, and be honest with yourself. It is probable that you already feel lonely and isolated. And will your children really be better off staying in an unhappy home?

You worry about not finding another man, but right now you are feeling worthless and unloved. Your self-esteem is low – it is only natural to think that no one else will want you. But as you begin to see that you are not alone, that you are not to blame and that you are an important, worthwhile person, all that will change. Once you have regained your independence, you may even decide that you do not want another relationship for a while.

Leaving may be taking a step into the unknown, but that unknown may be far more fulfilling than your life as it is. Ask yourself what you really want from life and how you think you can best achieve it: by going or by staying?

Melinda could not forget the good side of her relationship with Trevor, but I asked her to weigh up the good times and the bad times and see where the balance lay. I wanted her to try to work out in percentage terms how much of her life was happy and how much was unhappy. Exploring all these questions put her on the road to change. But it took time – three years, in fact – before she made the break for good.

'Once a fortnight I'd say, "This relationship has got to finish. I don't want it any more,"' she says. 'Then we'd get into this cycle where I would leave – or he would leave – and then we'd try again. He'd be very, very apologetic, incredibly comforting. And I'd go along with that. I wanted to be comforted. And I missed him. Still do – the charming, nice side, that is.'

Most women I talk to try to leave many times. They often say to me, 'I knew I should leave – but there were just too many obstacles in my way.' As we have seen, women are often terribly trapped and frightened, so it is little wonder that it takes a great deal of time and courage for them to summon the strength to go. And, as Melinda points out, they have no reason to feel guilty about that: 'I think that, when you are so confused, the leaving process is not something that happens quickly. Neither is it something that I think you should feel bad about when it doesn't happen, when you do cope.

'I think that, for me, going back all those times was part of the leaving process,' she says now. 'I had to keep doing it, because eventually, when I left for the last time, I knew that I had done everything I could. I knew I really wanted to leave and I knew why I was leaving. There was a stronger bond between us than I was aware of, and it was very hard. But I began to see that there was a definite pattern to his behaviour.

'He would flare up, get angry, hit or punch me – for no apparent reason. Then he would walk out, or I'd leave. I'd be very upset, but I would be quite firm. I would say to myself, "I've got to finish it. It's got to stop. I won't cope with it any more." Just when I'd start to feel a bit stronger he'd come around and be very, very nice. It was quite insidious the way he would creep back into my life. He'd be very charming. We'd chat. Things would be very calm, and I'd start forgetting the bad times. That funny thing about memory would start happening – when that whole sweet loving side of him came through I just got sucked in again.

'I'd go through a period of feeling pretty bad because in a way I had failed, but also I felt relieved as well, and I enjoyed the good parts, because there were a lot of good parts. But what happened in the end was I started to feel unsafe when he was being nice. A voice inside me started to say, "This isn't real. Okay, it's nice, but the niceness is a forerunner to abuse. And I know that's coming next." And that was horrible. That was when I started to face up to the abuse. The objective part of me that said, "I'm not going to accept this," came through more and more.

'Gradually, each time I left, I found I went back with less of me. There was a bigger part each time which remained separate – rational, I suppose. I became more skilful about speaking my mind. My objective self came through, the side that kept saying, "I'm not going to accept this relationship." But it was still hard. Each time I left I tried to be strong, and say, "This is it." But one part of me would say, "Come on. You tried to leave before and you failed."

'The last time I went back to him I'd been away for six months and hadn't even looked at him – but I still went back. I shocked myself. But when I went back that last time, it was virtually a formal relationship. We had nothing in common. I was so cautious, I remember he shouted at me, "You won't even let me get angry with you any more." That last attempt was so unsuccessful that I had no doubts at all about leaving for good, and I think perhaps I went back just to convince myself of that.'

For most women who leave, there is a turning point, and for every woman it is different. Laura took everything from bruises to sexual abuse – including James's infidelity – but what finally made her snap was when he hit her in front of the children. 'I finally said, "Right, that's it,"' she recalls. 'I'd got to the point where I didn't care how I was going to do it, but I was going to leave. I'd just had it. All I figured was: "This is terrifying, this is frightening, this is bad, and this is killing me, and I can't do it any more."

'What really gave me the strength to stick to it was that just before it happened he had gone away with this woman he was seeing, and he had actually left me on my own for a couple of weeks and I had time to think, "Well, this isn't so bad – this is actually a better alternative than being frightened all the time. I would rather have some peace and be on my own." And so when he came round to sort of try and persuade me that it would all be all right again, I was tearful, but I never once wavered and thought, "Let's try it again." I just knew I couldn't put up with it not working again. I just didn't have the strength to try again – that was the difference. And I also realised that I *could* be without him.'

'I can't leave'

When Rebecca weighed up her situation, she felt that she simply could not walk out on Ralph, at least until the children were old enough to leave home. 'After talking to counsellors and friends,' she says, 'I woke up to what Ralph was doing. I could see that all the things he did that drove me mad fitted into his need to control. But I still loved him. And he had never been violent. I wasn't scared of him, just worn down by it all.

'Once I accepted that I was abused, I knew that I *could* leave, and in a way that made me feel less trapped. I knew I had the strength to do it, but I felt that if I could make small changes, bit by bit, make him see that he couldn't grind me down with his moods and his insistence on making all the decisions, then I might be able to make it work. The important thing was that by *deciding* to stay, rather than feeling I had no option, I felt as if I had got some control back into my life.'

Many women, like Rebecca, are unable to leave their partners – because of the children, because they have nowhere to go and no money, because they are too scared, or because they simply cannot give up on the relationship. Other women leave briefly, but return after a period of separation.

Abused women find it hard to leave their partners because they are emotionally dependent on them and have almost become extensions of them. For an abused woman to lose her partner raises the frightening prospect of losing herself. So unless she can do something which will sever the emotional dependency between herself and her partner, it is unlikely that she will leave him.

It is important not to feel guilty for needing Charm Syndrome Man so much. Remember, even the most independent women have dependency needs and find it all too easy to fall for someone as energetic and exciting as Charm Syndrome Man. To free yourself from him, you have to develop new interests, participate in new activities and find new friends. Inch your way along slowly. You do not need him to be fulfilled. As one abused woman has put it: 'Don't worry, don't panic. You won't die. You won't be alone for ever. Leaving may be the hardest thing to do, but don't feel tempted to call him and start things all over again. He may be charming and wonderful at first, but then he will go back to his old behaviour. Call a friend, do some spring cleaning, go to the theatre, get drunk, but do not call him. The feelings of panic will pass. The pain gets less and less over time. Embarking on a new life is difficult, but you can do it.'

When they ask me for advice on how to cope, I tell them to remember that they will not change their partners (only the partners can do that). But they can alter their own responses to the abuse. The most important thing – as Rebecca realised – is to regain some kind of *control* over their lives.

I told Rebecca, 'Hard as it may be, try not to take his insults and abuse personally. Try to be objective. You know by now that his behaviour has nothing to do with you. It is his problem. Remind yourself you are not a slag and a whore, a lousy cook, a bad mother, a selfish self-centred hussy. Remember that when you first met he told you you were loving, clever, caring, fun to be with. You haven't changed – after all he still says such things during the phases when he isn't being abusive.'

I see Rebecca regularly, and recently she told me, 'I don't let Ralph's moods get to me any more. When he is insulting I try to pretend that what he is saying has nothing to do with me. He called me a stupid fool the other night because I'd ruined the dinner, but I just reminded myself that he was doing it to make me feel small and to make himself seem better.

'Previously I would have been feeling guilty for being stupid and inadequate, but now I tell myself that that is *his* view of things, not mine. The more I can reject his opinions of me, the less he is able to hurt me. I feel much stronger, much more confident because of it. I feel active rather than passive. I tell myself that it isn't okay for anybody to treat me the way Ralph does at times. No one has the right to dictate to you, to undermine you in front of other people.'

Though Rebecca is now able to challenge Ralph mentally, it is important for her – and for other women in her situation – to realise that physically challenging her abuser, or even trying to argue with him, will not help – it can even be dangerous if he is a violent man. Every woman has to judge for herself just how far she can show her independence before her life becomes more miserable or more unsafe than before. It is important to remember that even if Charm Syndrome Man loses, one round, he will win the next – because he makes the rules. He will simply start a new row or find another excuse to be abusive. He will argue until the small hours of the morning if necessary. He will not listen to his partner's point of view, or accept it.

It is far more constructive for a woman in Rebecca's situation to use her energy to build up her sense of self-worth than to waste it trying to change her partner. 'Remind yourself,' I told her, 'that Ralph is irrational in his criticism. He will do anything to prove he is in control.'

Charm Syndrome Man is what he is, but his partner can try to undo some of his messages, and in doing so feel better about herself. If he criticises her, instead of apologising, she could say, 'You may be right,' or 'I can see why you might be angry.' This tactic does not let him win (her first response implies, 'But you could be wrong!'); it is a way of possibly defusing the situation by denying him the chance to have an argument. It is a way of doing something positive, of taking control over the situation – whereas if she apologises and tries to justify herself, *he* remains in control.

It may seem such a small shift of emphasis, but it is quite a triumph for an abused woman to be able to say to herself, 'I am calling the shots here – he may not know it, but the fact is I am *choosing* to let him have his own way, rather than being bullied into it.'

I suggested to Rebecca that she could widen her interests and make new friends. Ralph might have a grumble and then forget about it – he might not even notice, some of the time. However, he might feel threatened by what he sees as her striking a blow for independence. What Rebecca had to decide for herself was just how far she could go before his negative reaction outweighed the advantages for her.

I also wanted Rebecca to know that she could always leave at some future point. And she did not have to wait for some incident which would make her feel justified in doing so. It would be enough to say, 'I've had enough' or 'I am unhappy.' No woman should ever feel she needs an excuse to leave.

A woman can plan for that day – if and when it happens – by doing little things, such as arranging for a friend to look after the children if she has to leave suddenly, keeping the number of a refuge handy, saving some money, even keeping a suitcase packed. She could improve her skills so that if she needs to get a job she is better equipped, or she could see a solicitor to find out what her rights would be if she decides to leave her partner. Then, if she does leave, she can do so from a position of strength.

'It's knowing you're not alone'

When women come to Chiswick they are amazed to discover that they are not alone: that the confusing emotions they experience are shared by many, many women, who have similar stories to tell and can offer them a sense of comradeship – whether they remain with their partners or leave them.

'If you knew you had somebody to support you, you might come to the decision to leave a lot earlier,' says Beverley. 'Because that's all you want, somebody who you can rely on who will support you, and help you through it. Not necessarily financial support, but emotional support. Because it's very frightening going to court, and the police coming and people talking about you – that's one of the hardest things to deal with. I mean we're all social creatures, and nobody likes being talked about badly.'

Hazel says, 'When you get to the stage where you know you *can* leave, you need support. For a long time I was in a terrible state. I was so frightened. I phoned the

Samaritans one night because I was going to kill myself. Everything seemed to get on top of me. I felt so lonely – even now I feel lonely sometimes. But I can cope with it, because the support is there.

'The hardest thing was that always, in the back of my mind, I was thinking, "What is he going to do? Is he ever going to let me go? Would he suddenly come back? Would he spring up in the middle of the night, and do something awful? Would he kidnap the kids?" And then things started changing. I don't know exactly when they changed, but the support was always there when I needed it.'

As Rebecca says, 'It doesn't matter whether you leave your partner or you stay, you still need to know that there is a lifeline out there, that there are people who can put you on the right track again, if you start to get despondent.'

'You have to get in touch with your feelings'

When a woman has lived with an abusive man, she will usually have been so caught up in a web of guilt and insecurity that she suppresses her real feelings. Now it is time to begin to acknowledge them, however painful. Until she is able to get in touch with those feelings, she will not be able to act. If a woman is unsure of them, how can she decide what she wants to do?

Sally says, 'When I was with Guy it seemed safer and easier to deny my feelings, but when we finally split up I faced up to how confused and angry and sad I was, instead of hiding all that. Once you admit to those feelings at least you can try to do something about them.'

Unsettling as it may seem, to be able to say things like 'I am frightened of the future,' rather than pretending that everything is okay, is the first step towards considering the new options open to a woman.

Rebecca found that getting in touch with her feelings was the first step towards distancing herself from Ralph's abuse. 'When he had said something particularly wounding, I made myself think, "How do I feel? Am I sad, angry, hurt, despairing?" Doing that made me less anxious, because I could see the effect his behaviour had on me, and I could take steps to alter my reactions.'

'You can't change him'

Melinda explains, 'The man will say, "If only you don't do this or that, our relationship will be better. But it *won't* be. No matter what you do, nothing will be good enough for him. No matter what you do, it will be wrong. You can go over hurdles trying to change things. But unless *he* is prepared to change, nothing will change.'

Laura says, 'I knew what was happening was wrong, always. But I wanted him without the violence. I wanted someone he wasn't. I thought I could love him out of it, make him happy, or whatever. And I couldn't. It just got worse and worse and worse. The more I put up with it, the worse it got. I put up with so much, making excuses, hoping it was going to work out.

'When I finally left, I'd tried and tried and *tried* to make it work – I felt as if I'd been doing all the trying and nobody else had, and it was just too late for him to turn round and say, "Let's do it again." And, in fact, looking back, I know bloody well that it would have just gone wrong again.'

In order to move forward, what an abused woman must ultimately accept is that nothing she does can alter the situation as it is – only he can change it, by facing up to his problem and genuinely wanting to change. And the hard fact is Charm Syndrome Man rarely wants to change. He will do everything he can to remain in charge, whether that means attacking his partners physically, emotionally, verbally, socially or psychologically. Just as she is the way she is, he is what he is. It is no use hoping that his charming loving side will one day reappear and stay. His behaviour will always be unpredictable. She cannot mould him into something that he is not.

If she asks herself, 'Does altering my behaviour stop the abuse? If I am sure to cook his dinner on time, if I dress the way he likes, if I avoid inviting family around when he is there, does it have any effect on his behaviour?' The answer is almost certainly no.

Instead of burning herself out trying to change him, an abused woman can use her energy in a much more positive way: by focusing on her own needs, and building her own identity. She has the right to object to her partner's behaviour – however much she may still care for him. It may not be advisable to do so to his face, but she can assert herself in small ways which boost her self-esteem. Changing the woman's behaviour cannot change *his* behaviour – but what she can do is begin to take control over her own life.

'It's not your fault'

'All the time, when I was living with Dave,' says Beverley, 'some instinct was telling me, "You don't deserve this. This isn't right, it isn't your fault," but every other part of me was saying the opposite.'

'It is so important to remember that the things that are being done to you are not your fault. They are not of your making,' says Melinda. 'I had no reason to feel guilty. It was Trevor – and my family, who wouldn't believe what I was going through – who made me feel that way.'

Accepting that it is not her fault is a vital step for any woman. As long as she blames herself, her abuser has no need to own up to his behaviour, and she will never be able to stop trying to make things better within the relationship.

A woman has to learn to forgive herself for her shortcomings. Everyone has them. Her faults have nothing whatsoever to do with his abuse. She does not cause it. He chooses to behave in that way. Even if he has affairs, she needs to tell herself that Charm Syndrome Man will frequently stray no matter how 'perfect' she is, because he must always boost his macho image. It is natural to feel that in some way she must have driven him to it – because she was not attentive enough, she was not good enough in bed or she had 'let herself go' – but as long as she crucifies herself with these self-accusations she will never be able to find a way forward.

It is important for an abused woman to free herself from the kind of downward spiral of guilt in which Melinda found herself. Every little blow to her self-esteem made her feel more and more guilty, sapping her energy as she tried to make things work. Then when they didn't she felt guiltier than ever.

As she puts it, 'I used to feel guilty when Trevor criticised me. He made me feel guilty because the marriage wasn't working. So I spent all that time putting him first and myself last, and letting my friends go – and then all he did was lose interest in me, because he said I didn't make myself attractive enough for him, and I was boring because I never did anything. The result was that I felt even more guilty.'

Many women are confused because, whatever they do, their partners make them feel that they have failed. They believe that their failure to reach Happy Ever After is due to some defect in themselves. As one woman said, 'I have always been outspoken and independent. I know I can be strong-willed. But I was like that when we met. And he used to say that was what he liked about me. That I had a mind of my own. So why does he put me down every time I say what I think? How come he wants me to be a different person now? Why does he make me feel guilty all the time?'

The irony is that Charm Syndrome Man *is* attracted to women who have such qualities. But once he is in a relationship he feels threatened by the very attributes he fell for in the first place. Now, if she behaves in a strong, independent way, he feels threatened, and scared that she might leave him. So he undermines her personality. He makes her feel unattractive, worthless – and guilty, because she thinks she has failed him. She feels she has lost her identity – and her marriage. Other people, outside the relationship give her similar messages, and the spiral of guilt continues.

A woman needs to recognise that her partner is controlling her in this way because (however unconsciously) he wants to feel bigger and better than her. He may say that everything which goes wrong is her fault, he may say that she has personality problems, that if she changed her attitude everything would be okay – but what he is doing is manipulating and controlling her through guilt. And while he is able to do so, she will be unable to act for herself.

The way out of this cycle of guilt is to start devoting time to herself, putting her own needs and desires to the top of the list, for a change.

'You have to think of yourself as a real and worthwhile person again'

'I think women definitely need therapy and counselling afterwards, because for so long you've been told that you are dirt. You can't just wave a wand and become a real person again,' says Hazel.

It is important for a woman to take one day at a time, to try to make decisions at her own speed. She could congratulate herself on each small success. For so long she has been denied the right to think of herself as a worthwhile person. Now it is time to try to look at things through new eyes, to be positive about herself, to say, 'I am important, It's time to pay attention to *me*. The very fact that I have coped for so long means that I am a strong person.'

She could tell herself, 'I am only human, it is normal to "make mistakes."' Or 'From now on I make my own decisions and, whether they are right or wrong, I'm not going to feel guilty about them. It is *my* life, and I don't have to live up to anyone else's expectations.'

Instead of looking back and saying, 'If only I had done such and such,' she could try to make a list of the ways in which her partner tries to control her. Once they are written down in black and white they may help her to see the situation more clearly and understand what he has been trying to do.

She could make another list of all the things she would like to achieve in the next three years, as a way of focusing on herself rather than her partner.

In a third list she could try to note all her positive qualities – however silly they may sound, they may make her feel better about herself. If she has all these good things going for her, she does not deserve to be so unhappy.

Making such lists is not trivial: the idea is to enable the woman to distance herself from her situation and see it clearly and objectively.

Re-establishing contact with people outside the relationship and breaking the isolation so many women feel is another important step in building self-esteem, because it will help an abused woman to realise that she is not as dependent on her partner as she may think. Women grow up believing that they need a man to look after them. So it is often hard to say, 'I can be myself. I can be independent.' But developing her own identity and assuming control over her own life is vital for a woman if she is going to free herself from the influence of her abusive partner.

Sally says, 'All the time I was with Guy I felt that my happiness depended on him. When we split up I felt lost at first, but now the wonderful thing is that I don't have to depend on any man to make me feel good about myself. No man can actually do that for you, you have to really like yourself first. Yes, it would be nice to meet someone else – as long as he didn't behave like Guy! – but I don't feel any pressure on me to have another relationship. I have other friendships, I go to the theatre, I read. I do all the things I couldn't do because he always wanted me to do something else. No way am I sitting around waiting for Mr Right to come along.'

That is not to suggest that the answer to everything is to substitute an abusive partner with a flurry of work and partying. That does not build self-esteem either. People often bury themselves in their work to cover up pain, loneliness, inadequacy and a host of other problems, but work only acts like sticking plaster: it covers up the wounds, it does not heal them.

Real self-esteem is about accepting yourself, warts and all. Being your own best friend. You do not have to become the head of a company, climb Everest or be seen in the hottest nightclubs to be important and worthwhile. Just 'being' is enough. Go your own way, find your own style. Just because the world seems to be saying, 'Be sexy' or 'Be a power dresser' or whatever is fashionable at the moment, does not mean you have to follow suit. If you do, you are acting, you are not being true to yourself. It might be fun to be sexy or powerful, but if it is not *you* then it will not give you any real sense of self-worth. A person with real self-esteem would say, 'It may be fun to be sexy,' or 'How fascinating to have all that power.' 'Isn't it interesting that people are all so different? But I am what I am. I'll go my own way.'

It is not easy building self-esteem when you live with a man who abuses you day in day out. Over time a woman begins to believe the negative things her partner says about her, and very often he is so controlling that she finds it impossible to focus on her own needs. However, as Rebecca found, doing small things which made her feel good about herself helped enormously, even if it was only taking a swim, having a manicure or listening to music. It is important for a woman to inch herself along slowly. She can try telling herself that she is not stupid or lazy and so on. Whether she stays with the relationship or leaves, she can build her self-esteem by doing things like cooking a nice meal, for *herself*, fantasising about a future in which she is happy, visiting a friend, having her hair done, remembering times when she felt loved and fulfilled, taking some form of exercise, meditating or contacting friends with whom she has lost touch.

As Laura says, 'It is so important to get completely away from the idea of the abuse, and do things for yourself, strengthen your contacts with other people and do things that you enjoy doing, that make you feel good and give you security – become involved in the outside world again.'

'You have to let out all the anger'

'For about two weeks after I left Trevor for the last time,' says Melinda, 'I felt the most intense anger towards him. I was consumed with anger. I started thinking about all the things that had happened and I felt very, very indignant. I relived it all and I felt I had been absolutely powerless. I thought, "How dare he do all those things?" I wanted to punish him. I wanted revenge. It was awful. I was obsessed and I didn't like those feelings. But after two weeks the feelings suddenly diminished, and I began to feel more separate from him. Once the anger had gone, I felt as if something had broken between us. I felt able to look towards the future without being so tied up with this man.'

Using anger constructively can play a vital part in strengthening a woman's resolve to free herself from her abusive partner. For so long she will have internalised her anger and her pain, unable to express her frustrations for fear of sparking off more abuse. Bottling up anger in that way can lead to stress and depression. It can often result in a woman taking it out on her children, friends and colleagues.

Being angry is a good sign. It is another way of showing that she is getting in touch with her feelings again, after years of suppressing them. Just telling people, 'I am angry about what he has done,' or saying, 'I am important. He has no right to treat me like this,' is a way forward.

A woman needs to know that she is not to blame for the abuse, that it is her partner's problem, not hers. Once she can accept that, she can see that she does not deserve her treatment and she can feel justified in being angry. And constructive anger plays an important part in rebuilding a woman's self-esteem.

* * *

Whether a woman leaves her partner or stays with him, breaking Charm Syndrome Man's control over her is hard. There will be times when she will falter – and, if she leaves, she may be tempted to go back to what is familiar, however unhappy that life may be.

However, if a woman can accept the reality of her situation and let go of the Happy Ever After fantasy – the belief that she can somehow turn her partner permanently into the reliable, loving and tender man she thought she had found – then she can channel that energy into creating a new life for herself, one in which she can find true meaning and fulfilment.

She *can* do it. As five of our six women can testify, there is life after Charm Syndrome Man.

I MUST DO IT

For Men

I would love to be able to tell you that Jimmy, Guy, Ralph and the other abusive men we have heard so much about throughout this book have admitted that their partners are not to blame, taken responsibility for their own behaviour and tried to change. But the truth is that, in terms of a way forward, abusive men have difficulty in facing reality. The very nature of Charm Syndrome Man prevents him from admitting that his behaviour is unacceptable. But unless all men – not just abusers – can wake up to the reality that controlling, dominating behaviour is abusive, that it cannot be justified as 'the way men are supposed to behave', then there will be no way forward.

Just as I asked women who are reading this book to look at their lives and their relationships and answer a few basic questions, I would like to appeal to their partners to do the same thing.

Apart from physically hurting your wife or girlfriend, have you ever threatened to do it, or intimidated her by shouting, swearing, smashing up furniture or harming household pets, as if to imply, 'You could be next'?

When you make love, are you still tender and loving, do you still want to make her feel special, or do you just satisfy yourself and forget about her?

Have you ever made her have sex in a way that worried her? Or accused her of being frigid if she does not want to make love? Are there times when you have called her degrading names and abused her verbally, put her down or ignored her in front of other people, and ridiculed her?

Do you forget that once you thought this woman was everything you ever wanted? That once you told her you loved her just the way she was? Now do you concentrate on her faults?

If she challenges you on *anything* do you accuse her of being a nag, always complaining, and ruining the relationship with her whingeing?

Have you ever come home from work to dinner and refused to eat it, telling her it is horrible – or even thrown it away?

Once you have children, do you pretend they don't exist? Do you speak adoringly of them to others but at home fail to notice them or help to care for them?

Or do you use the idea that men and women have separate roles to avoid cooking, cleaning, washing up and looking after the children?

Are you jealous and possessive? You may immediately answer no. But think about it. Do you try to change her life by preventing her from doing the things she wants to do, like going out with her girlfriends and seeing the people she wants to see? Do you open her mail?

Do you make promises to your partner then let her down? Are you unpredictable? Do you refuse to go to social events at the last possible moment, leaving your partner to explain your absence to others?

Do you accuse her of having affairs without any grounds? Or cover up for the fact that *you* are having an affair by saying that she must be paranoid?

Have you ever tried to interfere with her relationship with

the children – for example, sending them to bed on your return home, when you know she enjoys spending time with them, or tried to turn them against her by saying things like, 'Your mother is always spending too much' or 'Look what I have to put up with – she's always arguing with me.'

Do you overrule her when it comes to making the decisions? Do you think that *you* know what makes her happy? How often does she have the say in what you do, where you go on holiday, what colour to paint the living room, when to switch off the television?

Do you decide how to spend the money – do you ration it out and expect your partner to account for every penny she has spent? Or do you feel entitled to spend *her* money?

Do you confide in her, or do you exclude her from your feelings? Do you think that women should be intuitive and understanding, that therefore you have no need to talk to your partner? Have you become secretive, or do you actually lie to her?

Do you expect her to understand, forgive, and look after all your emotional needs – without feeling that you have to reciprocate? Do you think that these are feminine, not masculine qualities?

Have you ever decided to punish her for not behaving the way you think she should – for example, do you try to frighten her by showing your anger, or refuse to speak to her for days when you know she cannot stand your silence?

If you are arguing with your wife or girlfriend do you find it hard to concede that she might be right, or hard to accept criticism? Are you always on the defensive? Do you accuse *her* of changing – and tell her that is why you come home late from work so much, or go to the pub without her?

Rather than accept that you might be in the wrong, do you try to shift the blame by saying things like 'You don't know what you're talking about – you've had too much to drink,' when really you know she has only had one glass of wine?

Do you constantly remind her of things she 'did wrong',

and bring up old grievances whenever you get the opportunity?

Take a look at other areas of your life too. Do you put other people down and criticise them, so that you appear in a better light? Do you blame other people for everything that goes wrong, such as colleagues at work, other drivers on the road?

Do you have to win, to be the best: on the football pitch or the squash court? Do you want to be the centre of attention in the pub or at parties? Do you like to be seen as Mr Nice Guy – but forget to behave the same way with your partner?

Do you have 'real' friends, to whom you can turn when you are in trouble, or have you cut yourself off from other people, expecting your partner to fulfil every emotional need?

Have you ever threatened suicide, or vowed to hurt or kill her or the children if your partner says she is leaving you?

Do you find it hard to express your fears, worries, sadness, in any other way than anger or rage?

Are you jealous about possessions, other than 'your woman': your car, stereo, etc.?

Do you make sexist jokes, and talk about women as 'bits of skirt' or 'dumb blondes'?

Of course no one has a perfect relationship. We all say things we do not mean, we wound the people we care about most, we make mistakes – but look at this list carefully. Do you see something more than a yes to one or two questions. Do you recognise a pattern?

Does your partner complain about these things, has she left you for any of these reasons? Does she say she is frightened of you, or withdraw from you? Does your behaviour alienate her?

Have the children ever seemed wary, or asked, 'Why did you hurt Mummy?'

If the answer to any of these questions is yes, it

means that you are involved in a pattern of controlling behaviour, which – whether you know it or not – you learned long before you ever set eyes on your partner. It is not something which just happened one day – this kind of behaviour is something which has been encouraged and nurtured throughout society for centuries, as I showed in Chapter 5. Abusive men have learned that it is their right to control and dominate women, if necessary through physical, emotional or verbal abuse.

'Accept responsibility for what you are doing'

The first step for an abusive man – just as it is for an abused woman – is to face the truth. For the man, that means admitting that his behaviour is unacceptable and taking responsibility for his actions, rather than blaming his partner. Nothing that she does can cause him to behave the way that he does. It is no use hiding behind the explanatory myths, such as drink or drugs, stress or unemployment. These things may make him feel frustrated and angry, but they are only excuses – they do not cause the abuse. Many men have similar problems, but do not abuse their partners.

Abusive behaviour is not a sickness, nor is it caused by problems in a relationship. Abusive behaviour is about trying to maintain or gain control over your partner. As one man I appeared with on a television series on woman abuse admitted, 'You want control of your belongings. If you don't get what you want, you strike out. I have to have control around me totally so that I feel safe and adequate as a person . . . I never blamed myself. I might have been the assailant, but I never blamed myself. It was: "You made me hit you." It was never me.'

It is no use seeking other kinds of counselling such as marital or couples therapy until a man can accept the basic fact that his behaviour is about control. It is not the relationship which must change, but *his* behaviour, and while he is still controlling and dominating his wife or girlfriend there is no chance of building trust or communicating properly.

Accepting responsibility is no guarantee that the relationship will work, but understanding why a man behaves in the way he does is crucial. Stopping his abuse is the goal. And if the relationship cannot be saved, one way in which a man may accept his responsibility is to show it in terms of securing his partner's future. He could pay maintenance without being grudging about it, let her have the house and give the children a decent standard of living whenever possible.

'You are not alone'

Abusive men are not alone; there are many men from all walks of life, social positions and income brackets who behave in a similar fashion. Research shows that woman abuse accounts for 25 per cent of all recorded violent crime, and many, many more men emotionally abuse their partners and never figure in the statistics. However, that is no excuse. The bottom line is: what they are doing is unacceptable.

It is against the law for a man to hit his partner, even if they are married and the assault takes place within the home. And it can lead to murder. Remember that 30 per cent of murders in England and Wales involve men killing their partners. And while emotional and psychological abuse may not leave visible wounds it can drive a woman away, split the family and ruin everyone's lives just as surely as broken bones and bruises.

'You have a choice'

What is learned can be unlearned. Men must realise that they always have a choice. Everywhere they look they may be bombarded with the idea that men are the leaders, the controllers, the breadwinners, and that women are less important. The history books set the precedent and society promotes it in the home, in schools, in the media and in the way it denies resources to abused women.

But that does not mean that all men have to go along with these traditional views and attitudes (and many do not). They always have choices. They have the choice whether or not to accept those traditional attitudes towards men and women. And even if they accept them, they do not have to go so far as to abuse their partners to maintain their position. That is the second choice they make.

Their wives may be irritating, ignorant, unreasonable – no one is saying all women are angels. But a woman cannot *make* a man behave abusively. He always has an alternative. He can try to talk to her, see her point of view and not impose his views on her. As a last resort, he can walk away, go to the pub, call a friend. Or even get a divorce.

'Talk to people'

An abusive man who seriously wants to change can help himself by cultivating friends and contacts outside his relationship, rather than demanding that his partner meets every emotional need. Many men who feel depressed, worried and suicidal because of their behaviour find it difficult to talk to anyone close to them, but there are doctors, therapists or counsellors they could turn to, who will treat their cases in complete confidence. There are some specialist men's programmes in this country, but if there is not one available in your area, there are other sources of help such as psychotherapists and counselling agencies.

If a man isolates himself from outsiders, he is more prone to possessiveness and jealousy, he will suffocate his partner with his dependency and his controlling behaviour, and become more and more abusive whenever he feels threatened by an act of independence.

A man could ask himself whether behaving jealously is going to achieve anything. Even if she *was* being unfaithful, would being jealous help anyone? Monitoring her life and interrogating her about her every movement will ultimately have the effect that he dreads most. It will drive her away.

'She has a right to her own life'

An abusive man must accept that his partner has a right to live her own life without being dominated and controlled. He has no right to 'keep her in line'. And living independent lives need not interfere with the intimacy of a relationship. Of course, people who live completely separate lives can drift apart, but the kind of dependency on which an abuser insists is just as destructive. There is a balance, in which both partners accept the right of the other to be their own people, have their own friends and activities, state their own opinions, yet are still able to share their experiences and have an equal say in the relationship.

If a man cannot accept that his partner is entitled to live her own life, then at least if she decides to leave he can try to respect her decision, however painful it may be, and not track her down or pump her family, friends or children to find out where she is in order to harass her, or exert more control over her life.

He should not succumb to the temptation to use the children: asking them to 'Tell Mummy I love her,' or saying, 'It was your mother's fault we aren't a family any more.' He must accept that threats and further abuse are never the way to get her back. He may have alienated her for ever. She may never trust him again.

It may be hard, but the only course is to comply with the terms of protection orders and injunctions, and try to help himself by taking positive steps to understand the causes of the abuse and learn to deal with it in the future.

But on the positive side, it is not the end of the world. Even if the man must face the fact that there is no hope for the relationship, he may still be able to change his behaviour and begin a sharing relationship with someone else. Not only will his relationships with future partners be more fulfilling, but he will find it easier to cultivate real friendships and relate to other people in all spheres of his life.

'Stop using anger to control your partner'

An abusive man can learn that it is possible for anger to be kept in check. He must learn that it is not 'sissy' to discuss things, express his emotions and vulnerability, rather than venting everything through anger, violence and abuse. In the meantime, he should consider his partner's safety. If he won't control his anger, perhaps it would be best to consider a separation, until he decides to learn to deal with his emotions.

I would like to say to any abusive man reading this: take a look at your behaviour. Try to recognise the ways in which you attempt to control your partner. Ask yourself: are you really angry because your shirt is not ironed, or is the real issue something deeper? Is it because she has somehow transgressed from the role you expect her to fulfil? Do you treat anyone else in this way, or is it only your partner?

Just because you have been allowed to treat her in this way for a period of time does not mean you have to continue. You can begin to change the pattern by listing all the less obvious ways in which you might be trying to control your partner.

Do you interrupt her constantly? When she is asked a question, do you answer for her? Do you expect and demand more space than her in the home: like Guy, do you insist that your possessions or books are more important and therefore can be on show in the house, while hers are hidden away upstairs or in cupboards? Do you have your own office, den or workshop, while the only space she has for herself is the kitchen?

Do you ever bother to find out whether she wants to have sex every night, or is it just a masculine reflex action? You could try looking at sex differently, as a way of developing real closeness and trust. As something which is about love and tenderness, rather than the need to 'perform'.

Of course, there are going to be times when you differ greatly on something. But remember, a woman cannot be a mindreader: there is no point in losing your temper when she may not even know what is annoying you. Instead of exploding, 'You drive me mad!', why not start by saying, 'I think . . . ', 'I feel . . . ', 'I would like . . . '. Approach things in a way that does not instantly imply blame and criticism.

Things are never black and white, right or wrong. People are different and are entitled to hold different views from yours. Instead of digging in and trying to prove a point all the time, why not say, 'Okay, that's your view, but what I feel is . . . '.

It is hard to change a pattern completely. It may make you feel anxious, alone and unsure of yourself, because you no longer have that powerful weapon of anger and control to fall back on. But persevere, get support from friends or counsellors if necessary. Because learning that things can be worked out in a non-aggressive way could dramatically change your life.

One of the few men I have talked to who actually accepted responsibility for his behaviour and took positive steps to change was Lawrence, a bank clerk. He had been referred to a counselling group after the police had been called to his home because he had hit his wife. After two years with the group he admitted, 'The fact that I got arrested made me take a second look at what was happening. For too many years the general attitude has been that a man should be able to discipline his wife. That's stupid. The wife is a person, just like him.

'He has no right to discipline her any more than she has the right to discipline him. There are laws against this. There are laws against beating anyone, and too many times wife-beating is just seen as a domestic thing. Someone is being hurt, someone is being hurt badly, and the husband is getting away with it because it is a domestic thing. It isn't a domestic thing, it's an assault. No matter what you say about wife-beaters, in most cases he loves his wife and she loves him, but I don't know any of them who get violent with *other* people when they can't get their own way – only their wives.

'I think that somewhere in the back of my mind I thought home was my castle and I was the king. I think it's a case of thinking you are the boss, the big cheese, and people had better do as you say. That other guy, the guy I used to be, thought everyone else was at fault. He'd say, "They know I've got a bad temper why do they push me?" But no one else is responsible for my temper, they can't make me do things. When I realised that, I thought, "Hey, there's something wrong here."

'I wouldn't go back to being the person I was under any conditions. I don't want anything to do with that person. I still get frustrated, but when things are at a point with my wife where it is so frustrating that you know if it goes on any further there is going to be a problem, I just simply say, "I can't handle this, I'm not in any position to handle this. I'll simply have to come back to this and walk away right now." That is the most important thing.

'We still have disagreements. I still get angry, but it's what you do with the anger. I'm a long way from being perfect, but I'm more perfect than I was two and a half years ago.'

The bottom line for an abusive man is: if he wants to find a way forward he must accept that what he is really trying to do is control his partner. And that that is just not acceptable behaviour. He must understand that she has a right to her own opinions, that she is not simply an extension of himself, she is a human being in her own right, with a right to work and have friends and activities outside the relationship, if she desires. He has to recognise that he does not own her body, that she has a right to say no to sex and that he has no right to use force to make her submit.

He can learn to listen, rather than dictate, to be supportive, rather than critical, to discuss problems constructively, rather than resort to blame, name-calling or physical
assault. His goal should be to develop a healthy respect for
and empathy with all women, not just his partner.

Once he accepts all this, he can then learn how to act
constructively, rather than destructively, in a relationship.
He *can* unlearn what society has been teaching him for
generations.

For Society

'What's the point of intervening? They'll only kiss and make
up in the morning.' 'You spend all that time on paperwork
and then they only drop the charges.' 'He just needs to cool
off a bit – they'll be all lovey-dovey later. What's the point of
arresting him?' I must have heard these kinds of comments
a thousand times from police officers during the training
sessions I run as part of my work.

But there *is* a point to intervening, arresting . . . and
charging. And it is a major one: the single most important
goal is to stop the abuse of women, and one of the most
potent ways of showing abusive men that what they are
doing is wrong – rather than something which men are
doing behind every door in the street, as one abuser put
it – is to arrest and prosecute them.

In my sessions with the police, they come up with all
kinds of reasons why they cannot take such a hard line over
woman abuse. Not because they do not want to help abused
women, but because, like the rest of society, they are frequently hoodwinked by myths. Frequently they do not recognise the seriousness of the problem until they actually
see hideous injuries. Then they are swift to act. But what I
would like to see is a policy which urges them to move in
much earlier, to *prevent* broken bones and horrific wounds.

'It's a one-off – I don't think we should do anything if

he's only hit her once,' they say. But how do they know it is only once, when, as we have seen, both the men and the women deny and minimise what is happening? (As stated earlier, on average a woman is battered thirty-five times before she calls the police for help.) And even if it is only once, I point out, there *will* be a next time. And next time she might be carried out on a stretcher.

'If we arrest him, he could take it out on her when he comes out of jail,' is another objection. On the contrary, Canadian research shows that spending some time in jail often has such a devastating effect on a man (especially if he has never had a brush with the law before) that he is deterred from behaving abusively in the future, for fear of having to face that kind of humiliation and isolation again.

'But you can't put the breadwinner in prison – you'll cause even more hardship by breaking up the family,' people say. I would answer that the family is already torn apart by violence. How does it help a woman if her partner is allowed to stay with her and possibly kill her next time, leaving the children without either parent if he is convicted of murder? Stopping him now will save everyone from years of misery. And if he is not stopped, it is likely that she will leave him anyway – so the family will still be broken up. Despite government pressure to maintain the family unit, it must be recognised that a two-parent family is not always the ideal when a child sees its mother being systematically battered and humiliated by its father.

'It's time-consuming and costly to get involved in "domestics"' is another objection I hear in my training sessions. I would argue that, on the contrary, a strong policy of arresting and charging will actually save police time and money. If they do not arrest an abuser, they will usually find themselves being called out time and time again to the same house.

'But women don't want to see their men locked up' is another argument I hear frequently. In the short term, that may be true, but in the long term, it is the only way such women will be protected. Even some of the men I speak to acknowledge this. They accept that without such harsh measures they would never have changed their ways.

Woman abuse is always treated differently to other crimes. If a woman was robbed in the street, or her home was burgled, would the attitude be 'She wouldn't like to see the poor robber locked up'? In my view woman abuse should be seen as even more serious than other violent crimes, where strangers are involved, because the woman receives a double blow. Not only does she suffer the attack, but there is a terrible violation of trust – which is compounded by the fact that society does not really seem to care. And she lives with her attacker.

I do not like to see people thrown into prison any more than the next person. (I suggest it is the prison system that needs reforming and that is where available funding should go.) But it is dangerous to be sidetracked into saying things like 'He's as much a victim – it's not his fault, he's a product of a chauvinist society.' It is dangerous to say, 'He only needs counselling,' because research shows that this simply does not act as a deterrent in the long term. If men commit other violent crimes, they are sent to prison, so why should it be any different if a man attacks a woman in the home?

The sad reality is that there is no effective alternative to arresting and charging. Without such deterrents, what is to stop men abusing women for generations to come?

It is a policy which has been tried and tested in other parts of the world. In Canada the results show that it reduced the abuse of women by 25 per cent. In California the same policy reduced woman abuse by 60 per cent after the first six months. In one US city, Newport News, Virginia, there was a decline in the 'domestic violence homicide rate' from nine in 1984 to none in 1987, after they started a pro-arrest policy combined with proper training. (*Family Violence Bulletin 89*, vol. 5, no. 3)

As I also point out to police officers in my training sessions, arresting and charging is also important in that it educates people about the seriousness of the problem.

Such a policy delivers four strong messages: to the woman the message is that she is not to blame. She has not been a bad wife or mother. She is no different from someone who has been mugged or burgled. It shows her that she is important, that she deserves better and that she *can* regain some real power to put an end to her suffering.

Second, to the abusive man the message is that what he is doing is *wrong* that he has no justification for controlling women and that there is a price to pay. I know it is a tough price, but making men accountable for their actions will ultimately increase their self-esteem. After all, it cannot be good for his self-esteem for a man to beat his partner. Many men feel depressed and guilty about what they are doing but they do not know how to stop themselves. 'But there is such a stigma attached to being in prison – how can that help his self-esteem?' people often say. My point is that if we make such men face up to the reality of what they are doing, and why they are doing it, they may seek help to change their behaviour and therefore heighten their self-esteem in the long run.

Third, to society as a whole the message is that the abuse of women is unacceptable, criminal behaviour. Once that is universally recognised, police, social workers, neighbours, friends and family can feel that it is their right and duty to intervene when they suspect that a woman is being abused in the home.

The fourth message is to the next generation, to the children. They must be brought up knowing that violence towards women is not the norm, but a punishable crime. That there are ways of handling problems other than being violent and abusive.

'Just calm down, mate'

In theory police have the power to intervene when men abuse women in the home. The Police and Criminal Evidence Act of 1984 gives officers powers of arrest in cases where they have reasonable grounds to believe that an assault has taken place, or may take place, however minor, or 'in order to protect a vulnerable person or child'. It also provides for Crown Prosecutors to compel a woman to give evidence. A force order was also issued in 1987 by the Metropolitan Police drawing attention to these powers.

But in practice, rather than arresting and charging, many officers still say things like, 'Just calm down, mate,' or 'Don't worry, love, we've talked to him and he won't touch you now.' Little do they know that, once they have closed the door, many men take up hitting their partners where they left off. The order is not always being enforced at the level of the officer on the beat. Nor is the rest of the country following London's initiative.

The Home Office has suggested that an option available to the police is to caution men in cases which they consider are 'slight', that is where a man only slapped his partner or pushed her, where the man admits to it and where there is no previous criminal record or history of violence. In these instances they need not charge: cautioning is enough.

But cautioning is not enough. For a start, it often leaves the woman exposed to an abuser who is likely to be even more irate because the police have been called. In one area of London where a pilot scheme is operating, when abusive men are cautioned, they are in effect told, 'Go home and be a good boy.' If they do not harm their partners within, say, a two-month period, they will not be charged – but imagine the burden that places on a woman who may already be terrified and confused by her partner's behaviour. If he is violent again she has to make yet another call – and this time she is more aware of the consequences of that call. The pressures on her are doubled. She is also left in a vulnerable position, and may become a murder statistic.

Also, as we have seen, Charm Syndrome Man is rarely abusive every day. He may be perfectly capable of behaving charmingly for two months or more, but he will resume the cycle of violence some time or other.

And women whose partners have indeed been 'good boys' during the cautioning period and have then reverted to violent behaviour will be reluctant to call the police a second time. After all, what good did it do the first time?

Cautioning does not deliver a strong enough message that an abusive man's behaviour is unacceptable. Cautioning puts the crime on the same level as juvenile crime and shoplifting by elderly people (the main areas in which officers caution rather than arrest). Why are we delaying a real way forward by advocating such futile measures? In my experience, unless the cycle of violence is stopped as early as possible, it will only escalate – no matter how many cautions are issued.

The other problem with cautioning is that not only does it give police officers who are already reluctant to intervene a soft option to fall back on, but often police are not able to check all the facts. There is no central computer. How are the Manchester police going to know whether a man has previously assaulted a woman in Devon?

One case I heard about illustrates both these points. A man (who had been in the armed services) brutally battered his wife in front of his children and held a pillow over her face, almost suffocating her. Neighbours called the police, yet he was simply cautioned. What was minor about this case? No only that, but he was later discovered to have been charged with actual bodily harm against her in the past – but in a different part of the country.

Charging, not cautioning, *must* be the norm – no more of the 'Just calm down, mate,' attitude which results in abusers, such as Hazel's husband, being taken around the corner to the local pub by the police, rather than to the police station.

'We understand what you're going through'

Since a police officer is often the first person a woman encounters when she cries for help, the police need specific training in how to handle and understand the specialist nature of the problem of woman abuse. It is imperative that they take abused women seriously, and avoid implying blame by asking questions such as 'What did you do to make him hit you?'

Progress *is* being made. In 1986 the Home Office issued guidelines to chief constables stressing the urgent need for special training for officers, and special treatment of abused women. Crimes and complaints were to be carefully recorded, more female doctors were to be available to examine the women, and women were to be questioned separately from their abusers, with, if possible, a woman police officer on hand. Police stations were also to be supplied with the contact numbers of local refuges and sources of advice and counselling. The Home Office further recommended that, when abusers were arrested, their partners should be notified of their release dates.

Special domestic violence units have been set up in several London stations, to deal specifically with the problem of woman abuse. This should be a positive thing, and when such units work, they work extremely well. It is good for women and agencies to know that there is a specialist officer who can be contacted.

However, many of the officers placed in these special units have not had specialist training. In addition to helping women with their immediate plight, they need to be able to advise a woman of the services available to her – where she can find a refuge, how she can seek financial and legal assistance and so on, so that she has the means to leave her abuser, rather than struggle on with no one to turn to except the man who is inflicting the pain. In London many police stations have pamphlets or advice sheets available giving just such information, but this needs to be extended to the rest of the country.

Also, the units do not operate twenty-four hours a day. And the officers at the units are often busy with follow-up work so that the calls for help are being answered by officers outside the unit, at just the point that officers with specialist training are required. Specialist officers are often snowed under with cases, and have little support from the rest of the station.

In addition, these special units are set up at the discretion of the chief superintendent of a station and, if he leaves, there is no guarantee that his successor will support the scheme. There is no consistency, either, in the way each special unit approaches the problem. Some will place great emphasis on the fact that the man is a criminal. Others will encourage a cooling-off period and 'counsel' the women, rather than arresting and charging.

I do not want to knock the idea of special units, but I do think they could be staffed in a different way. Not every woman feels comfortable being counselled by a police officer. There could be trained counsellors available as back-ups to support the women, to free the police to concentrate on more specific duties, and also to train the officers.

Another alternative is a close liaison between police units and women's refuges. Funds could be made available to the refuges to help them to take on staff specifically to work with the police.

'We will prosecute'

Like the police, and society as a whole, the Crown Prosecution Service (CPS) is guilty of treating woman abuse as a less serious crime than other forms of violence. Crown Prosecutors are not prepared to take 'weak' cases to court, so they may start to press for cautions, rather than encouraging the police to arrest and charge in all cases. The result is that the police, knowing that it is more than likely that the CPS will reject 'domestic violence' cases, go along with this. The buck stops with the police, and women rarely get a chance to have their cases heard in court.

I would like to see alternative ways of submitting evidence, particularly in cases where women are frightened to testify or where their partners are threatening them – as in the Michelle Renshaw case. Under Section 23 of the Criminal Justice Act 1988, if a woman is afraid to appear in court her written statement can be accepted instead – but this provision has never been invoked in this country. However, in one case recently, the police set a precedent by submitting a woman's evidence on her behalf (though Section 23 was not involved). I would also like to see the CPS accepting other evidence, such as testimonies from doctors, police and other witnesses.

The Crown Prosecutors also need specialist training in how to deal with woman abuse, and they need to work more closely with the police and other help agencies.

Sentencing, too, must be appropriate to the crime. Violent men are constantly being let off with suspended sentences, probation orders and short-term sentences. In the case I mentioned above, where the woman was so terrified that the police were allowed to submit her evidence to the court in writing, her husband was sentenced to six months in prison. But when his solicitor appealed his sentence was reduced to three months, on the ground that the woman was 'a loving and forgiving wife'.

Sentences should be as stiff as those imposed for any other violent crime, not only in cases of battering, but also where a woman is sexually abused by her partner. And that means recognising that rape is as much a crime when the woman lives with her aggressor as when she is attacked by a total stranger. In fact I would like to suggest that we go one step further and pass a law which states specifically that 'woman abuse' is a crime which warrants severe sentencing.

Judges must stop persuading men and women to attend conciliation sessions; they must stop accepting undertakings from the men that they will not touch their partners, and instead they must issue injunctions with the power of arrest. If abusers breach conditions of bail, they should not be allowed bail a second time. And in all cases of woman abuse it should be the man and not the woman who is forced to leave home.

If we really want to find a way forward to a time when men no longer abuse women, then the police, the CPS and the judiciary have to stop denying the problem and delaying the day when they take positive steps to prevent it. They must all work together to show society that woman abuse is a crime and as such will not be tolerated.

'Shouldn't we counsel the men?'

Many people consider that the way forward is to set up programmes to counsel abusive men. When I tell people that arresting and charging reduces the abuse of women by 25 per cent they say, 'But what about the other 75 per cent?' and argue that the way to deal with those men is through men's programmes.

However, as we know, Charm Syndrome Man denies that he has a problem, so he is hardly going to come rushing along to enrol on such programmes. I would also argue that the reduction in cases of woman abuse may only be 25 per cent now but, if future generations are made to see that woman abuse is a punishable crime, that figure could be significantly increased in the years to come.

The truth is that the track record of men's programmes is not good. In Canada, where a whole network of such programmes was set up, the evidence is that they help only in the short term. While men are actually being counselled they stop being violent but, once the programme is finished, they go back to their old ways. The problem is that they go back into a society which has not altered its own views.

It can be dangerous to place too much emphasis on men's counselling, because it may stop women from leaving their partners if they think that when the men enrol for counselling everything will be all right. Police, too, might become complacent and stop charging if they think there is a men's group just around the corner which could take care of the problem. Judges might also be less inclined to give appropriate sentences if they are assured that the abuser is going to have counselling.

I would prefer to see money spent on training all professionals, not only the police, but doctors, social workers and counsellors, to respond appropriately to the men as well as to the women. However, there is a more immediate priority: and that is to pour all available resources into helping the thousands of women who are suffering, and into educating society, rather than concentrating on counselling individual men.

In an ideal world, once we have established an arrest-and-charge policy, challenged society's traditional attitudes, provided immediate help and resources for abused women and their children, made more people aware of the extent of the problem, then, and only then, could we begin to look at men's programmes – not as the sole answer, but in conjunction with sentencing.

'What's in a name?'

Before we can even attempt to solve the problem of woman abuse, we first have to recognise it. And that begins with the very language we use to describe it. The issue is not 'domestic violence', 'conjugal violence' or 'abusive relationships'. All those terms imply mutual abuse, and in doing so share the blame between the man and the woman. What we are talking about is 'woman abuse'. The abuse of women is about behaviour which is designed to control and subjugate a woman, through physical, psychological, emotional and verbal abuse, aimed at inspiring fear, humiliation, shame and guilt.

The very first step society has to take is to stop skirting around the issue with wishy-washy terminology. What we are talking about is 'woman abuse', and something must be done about it.

'Her needs are special'

Doctors, nurses in casualty units, clergymen, social workers and other professionals should be encouraged to report abuse, keep accurate records so that the extent of the abuse can be monitored, and help to educate the public by using posters and so on. We need to establish a system of co-ordinating the response of professionals, helping them to co-operate with each other at all levels and throughout the country.

People in such key positions need established guidelines for dealing with woman abuse. They also need to be trained to spot it, so that when women come to them complaining of stress, depression, dependency on drugs or alcohol, they can ask the right questions, to discover whether there is something more concealed behind these symptoms. It may simply be a case of asking some basic questions as a matter of routine, such as 'Does your partner hit you?' or 'Are you happy with your partner?' or 'Are you frightened of him?'

Such professionals need to know the things that counsellors in women's refuges know about the specific needs of abused women. Couples should not be counselled together, nor should a woman be examined in front of her abuser in casualty wards – how can she speak freely and without fear when the man who is making her life hell and terrifying her with threats is in the same room? Counselling the man and woman together also – very subtly – implies that she is in some way responsible, that she can do something about his behaviour. But that, as we have seen, is simply not the case. Men and women need individual counselling, which should focus on building up *her* strengths and unlearning *his* control.

The way a woman is treated from the moment she first asks for help is of vital importance. Her situation must be treated seriously, and her needs should be addressed immediately, no matter how busy the doctor, social worker or counsellor may be. It may have taken that woman months, perhaps years, to reach the point of picking up a phone and asking for help. If at that point the person she turns to is unsympathetic, however unintentionally, she may never seek help again. She may even end up as a murder statistic.

First and foremost, the woman must feel safe. When

she calls out for help she is often in fear for her life and for the lives of her children. In the eyes of her abuser she has committed the ultimate sin of abandonment. He may have treated her with utter contempt during the relationship, but the last thing he wants is to be deserted, because that damages his ability to be in control. The symbiotic bond between himself and his partner has been severed, the woman he has depended upon to make him feel a real man has left him. In this state he is usually very desperate, and frequently very dangerous.

It is at this point that a woman needs protection most. Her partner will try everything from threatening suicide to vowing to kill the woman or her children. Such threats must always be taken seriously, since in most cases these men have already proved just how violent they can be, and the reality is that many women are tracked down by their partners and physically attacked after they have left home.

However, many men use more subtle appeals: an abuser may try to charm the woman with professions of love and remorse, he will beg forgiveness and promise to change – if only she will come back to him. He may bombard her with letters or flowers. It should never be forgotten that a woman may still have very strong feelings towards her partner. However much she has suffered, it is rarely possible for her to be singleminded about leaving.

She will be torn by feelings of love, pity and guilt at breaking up her family, and in this emotional maelstrom it is all too easy for her partner to remind her of the charming, loving, caring side of his character, the side which she fell in love with and which she wants to return for good. It is all too easy for her to push the bad times out of her mind and to believe that he will change. The professional needs to be very aware of this heightened vulnerability when a woman first leaves her abuser and, if necessary, to take steps to help her find out about her legal rights.

However, if the woman does return to her abuser, even if

she does so time and time again, it is important to understand the dilemmas she faces, rather than blame her for going back. However much an adviser may disagree with her choices and decisions, they must still be respected.

In order to protect the woman as much as is humanly possible, confidentiality is vital, especially if a woman has not actually left her partner but is seeking advice on whether to do so. If her partner should discover that she has told anyone about her situation, she may be in more danger than ever.

What is also vital is that abused women should receive the right *sort* of help. Something as seemingly minor as the way a question is constructed can make all the difference to a woman. For example, if a professional looks at a woman's black eye and asks, 'Have you been fighting with your partner?', he or she is implying that the woman is, partly at least, to blame.

Remember that when women ask for help they are invariably ashamed, humiliated, frightened and prone to blaming themselves, since that is what their abusers have done. In this state, even the slightest hint that a doctor, counsellor or social worker is in any way sceptical about a woman's story, or feels she is in some way responsible for her situation, can drive that woman to desperation.

The woman already feels isolated and alone, she feels that no one will listen, belief her or even care. Her fears need to be dispelled, and she needs the reassurance that she is not alone, that many, many other women have gone through similar experiences, that what has happened to her is no reflection on her, and that, above all, it is not her fault. No woman should be held accountable for the behaviour of an abusive man.

If counsellors and other professionals believe any of the myths about the causes of woman abuse, such as that it happens because the women have masochistic tendencies, then, even though in the short term they may be able to offer women assistance, in the long term they will actually help to perpetuate the abuse by cloaking the real issue with excuses.

Abused women must be helped to understand that their abusers act the way they do, not because the women are bad or inadequate people, not because the women attract violence, and not because the men have had one drink too many, but because such men believe they have the right to control and subjugate them, a belief which is encouraged and reinforced by society.

Counsellors and other professionals also need to be aware that abused women are survivors and that, because of that, they will have adopted techniques of coping, such as minimising or denying the abuse. Like the hostages in the Stockholm bank they may have learned to survive by adapting their behaviour to avoid situations which may spark off the abuse. All these tactics are vital to their safety and sanity while they are living with their abusers, yet once they have made the break, once they are out of danger, it is time for them to vent all the anger and hurt they have suppressed for so long.

Because they are so used to minimising their pain and excusing their partners' behaviour, no one should be surprised if women gloss over certain events, if they hold back details or if, having firmly blanked out events which are particularly painful, they cannot at first recall them. Some women seem to have so little to say at first that professionals may even wonder why they are seeking help. It may be a long time before they can admit the full extent of the abuse, but they need to be encouraged to talk through even their most traumatic memories, before the process of rebuilding their confidence and self-esteem can begin. They need to be shown that the survival techniques they adopted, often unconsciously, were right at the time, but now that they are free, and safe, they can begin to be assertive and independent again.

Even when women move on, it is important for them to keep in contact with the professionals, if possible, so that they know that they are only a telephone call away from advice and support in the future.

'Take it from the top'

The government should be funding a national campaign to educate not only professionals, but the general public. We need to teach children about woman abuse, that violence is not the way to deal with problems.

We need to train teachers to look for tell-tale signs in the children. If they have poor concentration, if their performance is not what it should be, if they clown about and seek attention in the classroom, it could be that they are living in a violent home. Teachers need to develop individual programmes to help them to cope with such abuse. They may also be able to help the women.

Women must be made aware of their rights: leaflets could be inserted in child benefit books, and posters and literature could be placed in nurseries, doctors' surgeries, clinics and social services departments.

There could be TV and radio campaigns telling people that woman abuse is a crime against society.

A specific body should be set up to monitor research and co-ordinate the efforts of people working with woman abuse, organise conferences, put out information and advise journalists.

In addition to refuges, the government also needs to set up twenty-four-hour advice centres for all women, at which they can receive on-the-spot counselling and legal guidance. The government needs to provide nursery places, to enable women who want to leave abusive men to go back to work: it needs to give them better educational opportunities and to establish job retraining programmes.

People ask 'Why should the government have to do this?' My answer is that woman abuse is a serious social problem. It means that there are many women who are unable to fulfil their potential and contribute to society because of that abuse. And in the 1990s women are going to be needed in the workforce more than ever.

It is cost effective for the government to intervene, because eliminating woman abuse would mean fewer women living in bed and breakfast hotels, on income support, fewer children in children's homes or in care, less demand on police time and resources, less demand on housing and social services.

'How can I help?'

Neighbours and friends need to know that they can – and should – help if they suspect that someone close to them is being abused. In cases of actual violence the answer is always to call the police. Nobody is suggesting you should stand between a man with a hatchet in his hand, and his partner.

Many people, quite understandably, worry about interfering, but it should be remembered that 30 per cent of homicides in England and Wales are of women by their husbands (1982 Home Office statistics). A phone call to the police could save a woman's life.

It may be that a friend or neighbour can keep an eye on the situation, and wait for the right moment to approach the woman and reassure her that she has friends who are willing to help, that she has a lifeline should she require it. An abused woman often feels so isolated and alone that just knowing there is someone out there who cares about her, and does not blame her, may be the spur she needs to seek help.

However, it is important to be patient, to listen, and not to force her to take decisions until she is ready. It may be hard for an outsider to understand, but an abused woman is rarely able to walk away from her abuser without conquering fears and feelings of guilt which at times seem insurmountable. It does not help her to have someone constantly telling her that she should leave without a second thought. A well-meaning friend who criticises her for staying, tells her she is crazy, will only intensify her confusion, guilt and lack of self-esteem.

Running down her partner does not help either, as the woman may leap to his defence, or feel that there is something wrong with her for having chosen the wrong man. ('He is so bad; I chose him; so I must be bad too.') Instead, the most important thing to do is to assure the woman that she is not to blame, that she is not responsible for her abuser's behaviour. It is necessary to bolster her self-confidence and courage by giving her the credit for coping so well, to emphasise her strength, show her that she will be able to survive without her partner, and make her aware of agencies she can turn to for help, if and when she feels ready to leave.

If friends and family need information on how to help people close to them, staff at refuges such as Chiswick are always ready to offer advice.

'Women are just as important'

Arrest and prosecution is the most palpable signal now and to future generations that woman abuse should be stamped out, but it is not enough. Nor is it enough just to dot the country with refuges. If we are ever going to see any real progress, the root cause of the problem must also be tackled. If abusers are to cease the kind of controlling behaviour which they believe to be their right, society has to remove that sense of right, and in order to do so it must take a long hard look at the attitudes towards men and women and their roles which society fosters. And it must make some fundamental changes.

As long as women are made to feel inferior to men; as long as they have little representation in the higher echelons of power; as long as they have little access to highly paid jobs; and as long as they are taught that their sense of worth depends on finding and keeping a man, they will always be targets for abusive men.

This is particularly important in ending the emotional

and verbal abuse of women, since punishment for such behaviour is infinitely harder to secure than if a woman has broken bones to show for her pain. In many cases of emotional and verbal abuse even the woman does not realise that she has any right to complain. She may not even be aware that she is abused. She only knows that she is unhappy, and that she feels manipulated and dominated to a suffocating degree.

We need much more media coverage of cases of abused women in newspapers and on TV news – perhaps we should even publish a 'column of shame' listing names of abusers. In America the most sensational trials are actually shown live on TV – no bad thing, since it makes people sit up and take notice.

Maybe we should adopt an unusually enlightened custom followed in the north of England back in 1862, when men who beat their wives were made to 'ride the stang': they were carried on a pole or chair through the town or village, while everyone hooted and jeered. In many country villages, there was another custom: a serenade of 'rough music' every night for a week or two. The villagers banded together outside the offender's house, banging frying pans, pot-lids, buckets, and shouting, 'Shame! Who beat his wife – come out and show yourself,' and making up songs about his offence.

We also need to encourage equality of the sexes, rather than resting on our laurels and pretending that discrimination against women is a thing of the past. We must challenge the traditional idea that men wield the power and women are subservient, an idea which still prevails. It is this idea that acts as a springboard for the abuse of women. Since we learn it almost from the cradle – by listening to our parents and teachers and observing their behaviour, through children's literature, songs and fairy tales, and television programmes – we have to begin the re-education process early on.

If we teach children that they are equals, they are more likely to act that way as adults. We should teach little boys that girls deserve respect, that they are not just 'sissies', that they are just as important as men, and that above all boys do not have the right to dominate girls. They must not grow up to be controllers.

We can also teach children about anger – that it is not something uncontrollable, something which cannot be helped, but a bad habit, an excuse for behaving viciously, a cowardly method of getting one's own way, of punishing. Children can be taught that it is possible to be assertive, to stand up for what they believe and to put opinions strongly without resorting to aggression or violence.

In later life, boys who grow up learning that women have a right to their own opinions will be able to see that it is better to walk away from a situation than to use physical or verbal aggression. If, from an early age, boys and girls are shown that men have no right to be violent, women may be less ambivalent in later life should they find themselves living with an abusive man. Ultimately, they may find it easier to leave.

Children learn from their parents. Although, as I have mentioned, this is not the cause of woman abuse, when they see their fathers beat their mothers, or they are hit themselves, they receive the message that love and violence somehow go together, that it is okay to use physical and verbal violence to get what you want, that it is okay to try to control other people.

I believe that we should not hit children, either at home or in schools. We must teach them that assertion and discussion are always preferable to aggression. Both boys and girls must be taught that love and abuse do not have to go hand in hand. Boys, in particular, are already surrounded by messages which tell them to be aggressive, so being hit themselves only strengthens the idea that violence is acceptable.

However, it is pointless to try to show children – especially boys – that violence is wrong if all around them they see it on the television and in the cinema, and glorified in cartoons and books. Nor is it any good if they constantly see women being pictured in degrading poses in pornographic magazines and films, or being shown washing clothes and cooking meals in adverts.

Of course, not all women want to be surgeons, engineers, lawyers. The important thing is that women should have a choice about the way they live their lives. And men should also be able to stay at home with the children, without being ridiculed. Millions of women enjoy being housewives and mothers, and have no desire to do anything else, but the important issue is that they should devote themselves to being wives and mothers because that is what they want to do, rather than unquestioningly taking on a role for which they feel their families and society have groomed them. Paying women a wage for being housewives and mothers would do much to give them a sense of importance, as well as reducing their dependency on their partners.

Choice is what it is all about, and from an early age children of both sexes should be brought up to respect the fact that women – and men – have many choices about the way they live their lives. They do not have to be bound by a tradition which says men control and women obey.

We need to educate our society through the media, through plays, TV soap operas, books and magazines. We need to clear away the myths. Senior editors of women's magazines could start now by changing policy at top level to encourage feminist writing which highlights the dilemma of woman abuse. Commissioned work could take many forms – short stories, articles, novels, films, advertisements, even cartoons. Editors could stop rejecting or diluting material which does not fit into the received view of domestic violence and stop accepting unending stories of women's experiences, to the point of salaciousness.

In an ideal world we would discourage Page Three girls, pornography and advertising which shows women in a negative light. We could also encourage those responsible for producing children's literature and textbooks to portray women in a more positive light. We could do with some enlightened storylines in children's books. For example, mothers – whether humans, rabbits, bears or pigs – could occasionally be seen doing more taxing things than making sandwiches and beds. Perhaps Daddy Pig could make the dinner for a change. And in adventure stories perhaps little girls could have some intrepid adventures, while little boys could sometimes be depicted as having gentle, compassionate sides to their characters.

Curriculae in school should be balanced, so that girls are not discouraged from studying traditionally 'masculine' subjects such as sciences or engineering.

When these girls grow up, if they decide to have children, we could help them to make choices by providing decent childcare, better training and better employment opportunities to help them to go out to work if they want to.

Many women find it difficult to leave their abusive partners not just because they are emotionally dependent on them, but because they are also financially dependent. Providing better and higher-paid employment for women, better housing prospects, would also help to increase a woman's sense of her own worth, and the idea of leaving her abuser would become less intimidating.

The way forward for society is to aim at three goals. The main objective is to make abusive men accountable for their actions, but in the short term the priority is to provide refuges where women can feel safe and welcome and can benefit from sound medical, legal and financial advice. In the long term, the ultimate goal is to alter society's view that men are entitled to control women.

Life After Charm Syndrome Man

I began this book with the story of Melinda, who was 'devastated' by her husband Trevor's charm when they first met. Eleven months later, he hit her for the first time.

Finally, after twelve years of marriage, and three years of trying to make the break, she left him for good.

Hers – like those of all our six women – is an encouraging story. She left her job in the city and, with a loan, set up a small business which is now flourishing, so much so that she was able to buy her own house. 'I can't tell you the joy of that house being *mine*,' she says now. 'I know I can go home, shut the door and not be afraid of anything. I can switch on the TV when I want, the children and I can eat when we want and what we want. We can go out when we like. It is such a liberating feeling, it is impossible to explain to someone who has never gone through what I did with Trevor.

'Then, about six months ago, I met a man who I've fallen completely in love with, and he feels the same way. He's great with the kids and they've come to accept him,' she told me. 'He showed me what normal life should be – because I had forgotten what normal life was. I feel so loved and cherished by him. He treats me with respect – it is wonderful. He isn't at all violent. But the important thing is that I don't feel I *need* him to be happy. Having that time to myself has shown me that just being free and in control of my life is enough. This man is just the icing on the cake.

'I had always had the idea that what happened with Trevor never could or would happen to me. I would never be abused by a man. And I was. But that doesn't mean to say it is going to happen again, or that I was attracted to it, or that it was my fault. That awareness that it is something which could happen to anybody has helped me over and over again.'

Hazel is bringing up her two children on her own, and her self-esteem and confidence have grown enormously over the months. When she left Jimmy, she felt so physically bruised, psychologically scarred and sexually humiliated that, she told me, 'I felt that nobody would ever want me after what he had put me through. I felt drained, just drained. As if I was nothing, worthless. The sexual abuse

was the worst. It got to the stage where I couldn't imagine
enjoying love-making. Sexual abuse is a horrible cruel thing
to do to anyone. It stunts you emotionally.'

A few months later, she told me, 'At one stage I could
only sit in women's company. Now I can be with men,
but I'm always on my guard. Because of the way I feel,
nothing can develop, and I feel threatened if somebody
starts to like me too much. I'm all right as long as there
is no involvement.'

However, when I saw her recently, she was much
stronger. 'The thing to do is to think really clearly and
don't think that it is your fault and blame yourself,' she
said. 'It *is* difficult. Even now I've still got problems to
sort out, but it's worth it. I've now got my confidence
back, and I really feel as if I'm getting my life together
now. My children are so happy, I know I've done the right
thing.

'Once you're through, there's no looking back. I know
I'll never be abused again. It's wonderful to feel that I'm
clean, that this is *my* body, and I'm in charge of my body.
If I make a mistake now, it's *my* mistake, and anything I do
in life is *mine*. I appreciate different things now. And I like
me. For a long time I didn't like me. For a long time there
was nothing about me I could like. When you're abused
for so long, there's nothing left for you to like.

'Now I realise I didn't deserve to be treated like that.
Nobody does. There are certain times when the fear comes
back, but I can control it now. Once you come through
it, you're a stronger person. Life is just so good. Even if I
was only given a year to live, I'd rather be the way I am
now than the way I was. The days are lovely, life is so
lovely . . .'

Rebecca, as I mentioned earlier, decided to stay with
Ralph, at least until the children were older, but she now
has a part-time job at a local art gallery, which she loves.
Ralph made an enormous fuss to begin with, but she held
her ground. 'He hasn't changed at all, he is still as domineering as ever,' she says, 'but I have changed. That is the

difference. I feel much stronger. When he criticises me and gets angry I still get upset, but somewhere inside a little voice pipes up, "Remember it's his problem, not yours," and I cope.

'At the back of my mind I always know that when the children are older I *can* leave. It's as if I have a compartment in my head devoted to thinking about that day. I imagine doing absolutely everything that I want to do. It helps to get me through the grim days.'

Sally is happily married with two young children. 'For a long time,' she says, 'I didn't trust men. But Graham has great sympathy with women. There is no question of him being controlling, or dominating me. We talk about everything. He supports my work – in fact I think he even puts *my* work above his sometimes, which takes some getting used to after the way Guy behaved!

'I think it is very important for women to know that the bad times pass,' she says. 'You *do* feel panicky – I did. I thought I couldn't live without Guy. I thought I would never get over it. The temptation to go back to what was familiar was very, very strong. But no one knows what is around the corner – for me there was a new job and, eventually, Graham. You do survive and you do recover. That feeling of being lost does go away. And you get a tremendous sense of freedom instead.

'I remember one day I suddenly thought to myself, "I can do exactly what I please today. I don't have to wonder what Guy will say if he walks through the door. I don't have to worry what sort of mood he'll be in. I don't have to keep looking over my shoulder." And instead of panicking, I felt so *free*. I got out all the books I wanted to read, which he had never let me display in the living room, and I found all the records he wouldn't let me play in case they damaged his damn stylus, and it felt so wonderful. I got an almost childish pleasure out of it.

'Even if I hadn't met Graham, I know that I was happier without Guy than with him. Of course, there were good times with Guy, but the bad outweighed the good ten times over.'

Beverley has a new boyfriend, Mark. She says, 'When I was with Dave I could never just be me and express how I felt. I was always very careful what I said, in case I incurred his anger and abuse. I would always censor my behaviour. I was always looking over my shoulder. Now I don't have to do that. I don't feel that Mark likes just a part of me that suits him. Or a part of me that is going to behave in a way that won't incur anger or criticism. I feel valued. All of me. I feel accepted.

'A good relationship is one which doesn't take anything away from you. It leaves you a whole person, but in a connection with someone else, which can make you more of a person. Mark is lovely. Very easy-going. Sometimes I have a little panic,' she laughs. 'I feel this is too good to be true. I almost want to run away, in case it goes wrong!

'When I met Dave I thought I'd chosen the right man, so I keep asking myself, "How do you know now?" But Mark isn't jealous or possessive. There *are* a lot of similarities about the way I felt about Dave, but Dave was obsessive, controlling, whereas Mark is gentle, happy with his life. He's not dependent on me. I do worry, but my instincts tell me it is different this time.

'And you know the most amazing thing? Feeling safe in bed! Going to bed with Mark is so lovely because I feel *safe*. When you are in bed with someone you are at your most loving, but you are also at your most vulnerable. With Dave that was when I felt at my most unsafe. I never knew whether I was going to be loved or hurt. If I was awake, I'd always have to face sex, yet he was impotent, but for years I was never allowed to say that word. I used to think I'd love to creep up on him while he was having breakfast and yell it!

'Finally I'm accepting that it is okay to be *safe* with someone in bed. That it is inconceivable that anyone should be angry and violent and hurtful. It is a revelation. It is wonderful. On one occasion I just welled up and cried and cried. I told Mark how I felt and he was so surprised.

'He's listened an awful lot. A lot of people would say, "How could you stand it? Why didn't you leave him before?" or "Well, what must Dave have been going through?" Mark hasn't said any of that. In fact one of the first things he said to me was, "You're not responsible for his behaviour." I was really surprised at that! Because that's the most important thing to believe. Mark has never done any macho stuff and said, "What a horrible person," but he's told me on several occasions that it wasn't my fault.'

Laura is now living with Peter, who had been a friend of hers for many years. 'Peter didn't know about the physical abuse, but he was aware of the way James spoke to me, and he knew he was having an affair with somebody else, and he felt that I was getting a raw deal, although he never said anything at the time,' she says.

'Gradually we got close. But there have been terribly violent scenes with James. He was capable of driving up and down the street and waiting behind a parked car until Peter came back, then he'd set upon him and attack him. I felt terrible, because I had an injunction which protected me. James wasn't allowed to come to the house or intimidate me, or harass me in any way, but what he'd done was attack Peter in front of me. I felt as if he was taking the violence that I had had, instead of me – so we ended up going back to court again, and they said that the injunction covered harassing Peter too. But it hasn't stopped the threatening phone calls. He still phones up and threatens to kill me. It terrifies me. It has worn us down a lot. In James's eyes I had committed the ultimate in disobedience, if you like – I mean, if he saw our life together as trying to get me under control, I'd finally escaped and I was out of control.'

Of her relationship with Peter, she says, 'After putting up with so much, and finally making the break, I'm never going to put up with abuse again. Because of that I'm desperately untrusting of Peter, and I know that I've pushed him deliberately. I mean, not kind of consciously, but I know I was seeing how far I could go at times. I was saying, "Is this real or is he going to hit me if I carry on like this?" I suppose I had to test him, because I couldn't believe it wasn't going to happen to me again.

'I still can't believe that I am with a man who is gentle and sweet, and everything else. Peter couldn't be more loving, and we couldn't have a more wonderful love life, but I still can't be sure. I just don't know . . .

'I gather that James's relationship with the woman he went off with has ended in some kind of violent situation, which actually reassures me,' she says, apologetically. 'I mean, I'm sorry, but it does. It's a slight case of my rubbing my hands and saying, "Well, it wasn't all my fault. I didn't bring it on myself." Because I remember this girl saying to people that James was the most gentle man she'd ever met, and she didn't believe any of the nonsense about how he was violent.

'He had completely charmed her.'

Sources

p. 4 line 10: Andrews, Bernice, 'Violence in Normal Homes', paper delivered at Marriage Research Centre Conference on Family Violence, 15 April 1987

p. 4 line 17: Smith, Lorna J. F., Home Office Research Study 107, 'Domestic Violence: An overview of the literature', London, HMSO, 1989

p. 4 line 18: Police Monitoring and Research Group Briefing Paper 1, 'Police Response to Domestic Violence', London Strategic Policy Unit, 1986

p. 79 line 9: Dobash, R. Emerson, and Russell Dobash, *Violence Against Wives*, New York, The Free Press, 1979

p. 85 line 9: Jaffe, Peter, David A. Wolfe, Susan Wilson and Lydia Zak, 'Emotional and Physical Health Problems of Battered Women', *Canadian Journal of Psychiatry*, vol. 31, 7 (October 1976)

p. 85 line 13: Gayford, J. J., 'Wife Battering: a preliminary survey of 100 cases', *British Medical Journal*, 1 (1975) pp. 194–7

p. 85 line 17: Hilberman, Elaine, and Kit Munson, 'Sixty Battered Women', *Victimology*, 2 (1977), p. 469

p. 98 line 28: Lifton, Robert Jay, *Boundaries: Psychological Man in Revolution*, New York, Vintage Books/Random House, 1969

p. 112 line 32: Stark, Evan *et al*, 'Wife Abuse in the Medical Setting', Rockvile, Md: National Clearinghouse on Domestic Violence, 1981

p. 112 line 34: Dobash, R. Emerson, and Russell Dobash, *op cit*

p. 136 line 16: Stanworth, Michelle, *Gender and Schooling: A Study of Sexual Divisions in the Classroom*, London, Hutchinson, 1983

p. 138 line 27 : Weitzman, Lenore J., 'Sex Role Socialization in Picture Books for Preschool Children', *American Journal of Sociology*, vol. 77, 6, p. 1125

p. 139 line 3: Souhami, Diana, *A Woman's Place: The Changing Picture of Women in Britain*, London, Penguin, 1986

p. 142 line 4: Sanford, Linda Tschirhart, and Mary Ellen Donovan, *Women and Self-Esteem*, New York, Penguin, 1984

p. 182 line 31: Family Violence Bulletin 89, vol. 5, 3, Family Violence Research and Treatment Program, University of Texas

Other works mentioned in the text

Cobbe, Frances Power, 'Wife Torture in England', *The Contemporary Review*, London 1878

Fedders, Charlotte and Laura Elliot, *Shattered Dreams*, New York, Harper and Row, 1987

Horley, Sandra, *Love and Pain: A Survival Handbook for Women*, London, Bedford Square Press, 1988

Lacey, Robert, *Princess*, London, Hutchinson, 1982

Martin, Del, *Battered Wives*, New York, Pocket Books, 1983

Mill, John Stuart, *The Subjection of Women* (introduction by Wendell Robert Carr), Cambridge, Massachusetts, MIT Press, 1970

Roy, Maria, *The Abusive Partner: An Analysis of Domestic Battering*, New York, Van Nostrand Reinhold Company Inc., 1982

Sinclair, Deborah, *Understanding Wife Assault: A Training Manual for Counsellors and Advocates*, Ontario Ministry of Community and Social Services, 1985

Turner, Tina, *I, Tina*, Harmondsworth, Viking, 1986

Further Reading

Caplan, Paula, *The Myth of Women's Masochism*, New York, E. P. Dutton, 1985

Dworkin, Andrea, *Our Blood*, London, The Women's Press, 1976
— *Pornography*, London, The Women's Press, 1982

Edwards, Susan, *Policing 'Domestic Violence'*, London, Sage, 1989

Goldhor, Harriet Lerner, *The Dance of Anger*, New York, Harper and Row, 1985

Halpern, Howard M., *How to Break Your Addiction to a Person*, New York, Bantam, 1982

Hoffman, Susanna, *Men Who Are Good For You and Men Who Are Bad*, Berkeley, California, Ten Speed Press, 1987

Horley, Sandra, *Love and Pain: A Survival Handbook for Women*, London, Bedford Square Press, 1988

Martin, Del, *Battered Wives*, New York, Pocket Books, 1983

NiCarthy, Ginny, *Getting Free: A Handbook for Women in Abusive Relationships*, Seattle, The Seal Press, 1982

Russell, Diana E. H., *Rape in Marriage*, New York, Macmillan, 1982

Russianoff, Penelope, *Why Do I Think I Am Nothing Without a Man?*, New York, Bantam, 1984

Sanford, Linda Tschirhart, and Mary Ellen Donovan, *Women and Self-Esteem*, New York, Penguin, 1984

Walker, Lenore E., *The Battered Woman*, New York, Harper and Row, 1979
— *Terrifying Love*, New York, Harper and Row, 1989

Yllo, Kersti, and Michele Bograd, *Feminist Perspectives on Wife Abuse*, Newbury Park, California, Sage, 1988